THE
FISHING
TACKLE
CATALOG

THE
FISHING
TACKLE
CATALOG

A Sourcebook for the Well-Equipped Angler

Herbert A. Schaffner

GALLERY BOOKS

An Imprint of W.H. Smith Publishers, Inc.
112 Madison Avenue
New York, New York 10016

A FRIEDMAN GROUP BOOK

Published by GALLERY BOOKS
An imprint of W.H. Smith Publishers, Inc.
112 Madison Avenue
New York, New York 10016

ISBN 0-8317-3372-1

THE FISHING TACKLE CATALOG:
A Sourcebook for the Well-Equipped Angler
was prepared and produced by
Michael Friedman Publishing Group, Inc.
15 West 26th Street
New York, NY 10010

Editor: Tim Frew
Art Director/Designer: Robert W. Kosturko
Photography Editor: Christopher C. Bain
Photo Researcher: Daniella Jo Nilva
Production Manager: Karen L. Greenberg
Layout: Deborah Kaplan
Typeset by BPE Graphics, Inc.
Color separations by Kwong Ming Graphicprint Co.
Printed and bound in Hong Kong by Leefung-Asco Printers, Ltd.

All prices listed in THE FISHING TACKLE CATALOG are quoted in U.S.
dollars. The prices are accurate at the time of publication, but
are subject to change.

I shall stay him no longer than to wish a
rainy evening to read this following
discourse; and that if he be an honest
angler, the east wind may never blow when
he goes a-fishing.

Izaak Walton, *The Compleat Angler*

TABLE OF CONTENTS

The Situational Angler

The domain of angling is divided into three parts: saltwater, freshwater, and fly fishing. As most fly-fishermen will tell you, the tools and skills of fishing with a fly rod are unlike those of any other sort of angling. One can fly-fish in fresh or saltwater, but the complex techniques and entomological and ichthyological knowledge (that is, knowledge of what insects trout eat, and when and why) required of fly-fishermen set this sport apart from other forms of fresh and saltwater angling. We will discuss fly tackle and fly-fishing in a separate section.

But leave no doubt about it. The fresh and saltwater angler can bring an endless array of tackle, tools, and rigs to the job of catching fish. Each angler's tackle not only reveals how that angler likes to fish—location, quarry, activity—but also a little about the angler's character traits. The angler who flails about with expensive equipment and little knowledge draws suspicion. Trust lies with older tackle that has lasted the years. There is nobility in casting for large fish with light tackle, which gives the quarry a fair chance of escape, and, yes, is more satisfying if the fish is landed.

But fishing stands as one of the most democratic of activities. There are as many ways to fish as there are fishermen, and the immense variety of fresh and saltwater habitat available to Americans and Canadians means that virtually everyone has access to public waters. One angler may like catching rainbows with a clump of worms drifted on the lake bottom. Another may prefer tempting them to the surface with floating dry flies. One surf caster may believe a live crab will be effective; another at the same spot may believe the stripers are hitting on the surface, and cast to them with a large surface plug. For some, nothing beats a long summer afternoon pulling a heap of crappies from a local river; others save pennies all winter for a week-long float trip down a blue-ribbon Montana trout stream. Just as a person's desire to fish in various ways is limited only by the imagination, the need to spend money is limited only by how cheap or lavish one chooses to be. An angler may spend very little and still enjoy the sport, unless, of course, he or she is determined to fish for steelhead in Alaska. Even Atlantic salmon fishing in Canada is now inexpensive.

The world of fishing tackle is a great, sprawling, open market offering thousands of products and spanning thousands of needs. No income is excluded. Products are relatively cheap compared to the tools involved in hunting, skiing, mountaineering, and other outdoor sports. Most varieties of tackle are extremely accessible, with most moderate-sized towns offering a tackle shop or two. Catalogs proliferate and are generally well-written.

Saltwater fishing is slightly less accessible and more expensive than freshwater fishing. Whether tuna off Montauk, Long Island, marlin off Bimini, coho salmon off Astoria, Oregon, or sailfish near Hawaii, many of the prize oceanic game fish are caught or found by professional fishing captains and guides who know the complex ocean fishing waters. Saltwater species must battle currents, predators, and weather, swim longer distances, and work harder to get a meal—which makes them stronger and faster than their freshwater cousins. This requires heavier, stronger, and more expensive tackle.

Most first time and novice saltwater anglers pay up and rent a space on a boat, with a large or small group for varying amounts of time and varying sorts of fish, depending on the money being spent. Most people have been exposed to saltwater fishing on charter boats. This is the great middle-class of saltwater fishing, compared to the high-rolling executives and millionaires who live for weeks on high-tech big-game cruisers hunting marlin, tuna, and other champions of the sea.

The low-rent district is found on the beach piers, bridges, and jetties where the casual fishermen can jig or use live bait to catch fluke and other bottom dwellers. Some folks own their own boats, and chase their local saltwater game fish on Saturday afternoons. The most demanding form of saltwater fishing is surf casting, which deserves respect—and gets it. Unlike boat fishermen, surf casters make their own decisions about how they will fish. A good knowledge of the migratory and feeding habits of the prey is crucial.

© C. Stork/FPG International

© Greg Vaughn/Tom Stack & Associates

In its association with the vastness and complexity of the sea, and the swift, predatory creatures that live there, saltwater fishing and its tackle can be intimidating. THE FISHING TACKLE CATALOG will act as your Virgil to guide you through the bewildering Dantean levels of saltwater tackle.

While saltwater fishing is like a feudal kingdom with clearly defined levels of expertise and respectability, freshwater fishing is a sprawling democracy of fishing styles and

Opposite page: Inexperienced anglers will find that charter boats captained by professional fishing guides offer the swiftest route to success in catching pelagic saltwater gamefish. Above: Surf casting offers anglers the extraordinary opportunity to hook saltwater gamefish "at field level," where he or she must bring bluefish, stripers, or other aggressive predators to the sand without the leverage of a boat. Left: Marlin fishing in Hawaii is always a thrill.

methods that spans everything from bottom fishing with doughballs for catfish to trolling herring in the Great Lakes for salmon. Most of us learned to fish in the local creek, pond, or lake using worms for sunnies and bluegills, or hooking up breadballs to catch little trout, which we brought up for Mom to cook for supper. But as anglers mature, they inevitably dream of larger fish and trophies for the den wall.

The rise in popularity of bass fishing culminated in its transition to a professional sport, with pro bass anglers competing for thousands of dollars in prize money every year, endorsing fishing tackle of all kinds, and starting their own cable television programs where they toss spinner baits from a boat and haul in 'hawgs while light country music plays on the soundtrack.

For many fishermen, trout, salmon, and steelhead are the pinnacle in angling sport and its most prestigious trophies. These fish are beautiful works of Nature's hand that require clear, clean mountain streams and lakes rich with oxygen to survive. They are difficult to catch by fly or other artificial means and are worthy adversaries once hooked.

The elusive muskie and populous northern pike are sought by anglers in the rivers and lakes of Canada and the northern United States. Guides and boatmen lead thousands of fishermen to the hot spots where the toothy gamers can be caught. The savage strikes and sheer power of these fish make them popular targets. They deliver to the angler a sense of primordial satisfaction in taming a supreme underwater predator.

Many other fish have their fans—walleye, lake trout, perch, catfish and carp, sauger, and smallmouth bass—and they are caught from a vast armada of boats on every pond, stream, and lake imaginable, and often caught from a comfortable log on the bank. Freshwater fishing is a regional sport, with anglers adopting local gamefish as their favorite prey.

THE FISHING TACKLE CATALOG will spill the cornucopia of America's freshwater tackle in its endless variety. It will pass along the wisdom of leading angling experts, both conventional and unconventional, and relate mouth-watering angling adventures

© Jeff Schultz

© Spencer Swanger/Tom Stack & Associates

Far left: *For trout and salmon anglers, Alaska offers the most abundant gamefish waters in North America.* **Above:** *Pure, cold Rocky Mountain waters bring anglers to the top of North America where the quarry includes rare strains of trout, abundant char, whitefish, Dolly Varden, and landlocked salmon.* **Left:** *A quiet freshwater stream is within reach for most every family. Afternoons of plunking for sunnies and catfish often lead to plans of catching larger fish in more distant waters.*

as experienced by some very interesting and prominent Americans.

The panorama of tackle types and models described is available in retail tackle shops and through the mail in various catalogs. Each of the book's "tackle shops"—whether saltwater, freshwater, or fly—arrange tackle not only by type, but by price and value received for that price. Like everyone, today's fisherman wants value for the dollar. The "Best Quality" showcases feature the best tackle you can buy, period; the "Best Value" selections sample high-quality fishing items available at eminently affordable prices; those products selected as "Best for the Beginner" represent those cheaper makes and models still manufactured with quality, lasting parts.

Most of the tackle goods listed in THE FISHING TACKLE CATALOG are priced in the middle range and selected for the premium level of quality workmanship and innovation offered for the cost. But never buy equipment based solely on price. Even if you're starting out, poor equipment can ruin the sport before you've caught a fish: All the

equipment listed in THE FISHING TACKLE CATALOG is worthy of your trust. No junk here. If you have money to spend, and experience to back up your purchase, be sure you know what precise sizes, weights, and models fit your kind of fishing before spending a lot of money.

As you review the name-brand tackle, lures, and accessories presented in the showcases throughout the book, remember that the selections represent a sample of the tackle available to today's fisherman. Items chosen for "display" will generally reflect the latest innovations in design, construction materials, and sizing currently marketed by tackle manufacturers. Therefore, a large share of the final selections in this book are drawn from new product lines. Like any technology, fishing tackle design is influenced by innovation, and every successful departure quickly becomes a standard feature on most models. The most successful technological changes are those that make it easier not only for an angler to catch fish, but also for the angler to have fun. The less intrusive a piece of tackle, the more popular it will be.

Most fly anglers protect their rods with carrying cases. These by Umpqua are among the best.

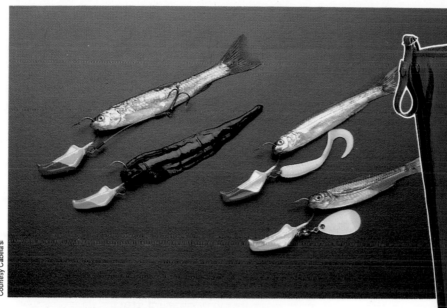

Courtesy Cabela's

Cabela Walking Jigs: *deadly on walleye*

Courtesy Cabelas

Colorado trolling and spinning blades for salmon, trout, pike, and walleye rigs

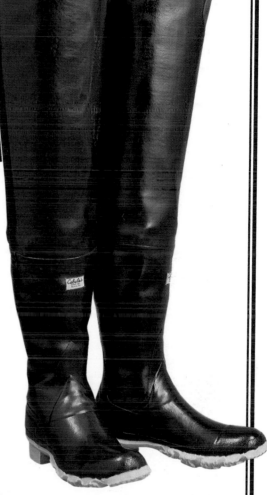

Cabela's Custom Ankle Hip Boots

The Daiwa Executive Spinning Case

Because fighting and landing the hooked fish provides the peak experience in angling, nothing is more important to the pleasure of fishing than choosing the rods, reels, and lines that match the size of the fish you expect to catch. As you consider purchase choices, remember that the tackle you buy should offer fair fight to the size of fish you usually catch—not to the extraordinarily large specimens you may net a few times in a season.

Landing large fish on light tackle is the essence of the angling sport. This observation lies at the heart of what I call the "situational principle" of fishing and fishing tackle. The more ways the angler's tackle matches the specific challenges and details of each angling situation, the more fish the angler will catch, and—far more importantly—the more he will enjoy the sport.

Successful anglers assemble tackle outfits that allow the mechanics of fishing to proceed naturally, even automatically. This enables them to concentrate entirely on catching fish. Each species available to the angler lives in a different water habitat, and different makes of rods and reels are more effective for different bodies of water, subsurface

© M. Timothy O'Keefe/Tom Stack & Associates

© Tom Stack/Tom Stack & Associates

Opposite page bottom: *Narrow, fast-moving, trout streams require pinpoint casting accuracy and absolute stealth from the fly-fisherman.* Left: *Lakes, reservoirs, and impoundments in the Southern United States yield champion largemouth bass to the angler who can read these vast stretches of water and find bass habitat.* Below: *Portable "belly boats" allow fly fishermen to fish gorgeous trout water like this easily and in silence.* Right: *Brook trout country.*

© Frank S. Balthis

© Hanson Carrol/FPG International

terrains, currents, and casting areas. Of course, the same is true of lines, leaders, lures, and terminal tackle.

When the angler is pursuing brook trout in shallow, narrow streams with brushy banks, for example, his tackle should make short, quick, accurate, no-snag casting as easy as possible. The size of his outfit should allow the smaller brook trout or rock bass a fair and challenging fight. His lures should imitate food that brookies find in that particular environment.

When the angler is fishing for steelhead in a large, cold Oregon river, he will be trying to locate 15- to 20-pound, muscular, sea-run, rainbow trout in wide, deep water. Steelhead position themselves in holes along the river bed where they feed on crustaceans and fish that pass close to their holding spots. The angler must deliver a bait or lure along the bottom of the river close to a holding fish—for river-run steelhead are not aggressive feeders when preparing to spawn. If the angler hooks up the fish, his reel must be strong enough to check the steelhead's long runs, and wear down the fish's strength.

The situational angler therefore chooses a 9- to 10-foot bait-casting rod of reinforced graphite for a combination of strength and lightness that helps ease casting fatigue. Preferably, the rod should have very fast action to help feel the tentative nibbles of the disinterested fish. The angler will also need the cranking power of a large bait-casting reel against the sea-run strength of the steelhead. The reel should be strung with 250 feet (plenty of line because the river is wide and deep) of 12-pound test monofilament with high tensile strength and good shock absorption to withstand the shock of the fish's initial run. The angler raises the stakes of the challenge with light test: it means he will have to play the steelhead carefully, using the entire river to tire the fish before bringing him to the net.

The steelhead in this Oregon river are known to eat the large freshwater shrimp that burrow among the rocks on the bottom. Our situational angler decides to use live shrimp, rigged on a large Mustad beak hook below a swivel and small slip sinker just heavy enough to drag the bait along river bottom. He will slowly bottom-troll the bait in a rowboat, which allows the current to impart a natural action to the bait. The boat gives the angler mobility on the large river. He has matched his tackle to his particular fishing situation.

This book will help you apply the "situational principle" to your own fishing life. If you're starting from scratch, you'll find good information here on how tackle components fit various fishing situations. As you add new elements to your outfit, THE FISHING TACKLE CATALOG will provide guidelines for mating rod and reel, line sizes, lure weights, and accessories.

All fishermen, believe it or not, are members of the species Homo sapiens, and possess the power of reason. Fish do not. Therefore, all advantage lies with the thinking angler.

Unbeatable freshwater fishing excitement: drift-fishing for the acrobatic, steelhead on the Alsea River in Oregon. Right: Fly casting for steelhead requires not only patience but thorough knowledge of river conditions, a working familiarity with the history of local spawning runs, and successful fly patterns.

CHAPTER TWO

Saltwater Tackle

Saltwater fishing is catagorized by sense of place: beaches and surf, estuaries and causeways, shallow flats, and deep open water. Perhaps the cheapest and most challenging way to pull cruisers out of the briny is to surf cast. As the name implies, it is done from beaches and jetties. From Kennebunkport, Maine to Newport, Rhode Island, and Narrangsett, Long Island to Manasquan, New Jersey, surf casters fire their tin squids and pencil poppers beyond the foam to the deep gulleys and fish-rich rips of the Atlantic for bluefish, stripers, weakfish, and more. On the West Coast, surf fishermen do similar work, in search of striped bass, jack crevalle, and yellowfin tuna. As you will discover if you hoist the tall surf-casting rod into action, blues provide the surf caster with his most exciting sport. Pound-for-pound, no ocean fish can beat these savage feeding machines for blistering runs and sheer lust for the strike.

Surf casting means saltwater angling without the advantages and comforts of a large boat. It preserves the one-on-one purity of the fisherman's duel with his prey. It is highly popular with veteran anglers, who prefer heavy saltwater spinning and surf spinning tackle for their work.

To be fair, search-and-destroy cruising on the bounding main for big game delivers high satisfaction when executed fairly and properly. The fish can be so big that the angler's imagination will almost refuse to accept it. You can't deny the visceral pleasure of battling and defeating a fish larger than the compact car you drove to the marina. The valiant beauty of a sailfish, marlin, or dolphin leaping and running in the last fight of his life demonstrates the extraordinary qualities of the hooked creature soon to be gaffed and sent to the fillet knife. Big fish present a substantial challenge to the stamina and back muscles of the angler in the fighting chair. Deep-sea fishing requires its own special category of "boat tackle," and is largely bought by fishing professionals.

Fishing for tarpon, bonefish, trevally, barracuda, and permit is done largely in tidal estuaries, rivers, and "flats"—the vast shallow coastal spans of warm tidal waters surrounding island chains in the Caribbean and Southern Atlantic. Aficionados of flats-fishing prefer light saltwater tackle, either spinning or bait casting with sensitive tips for bonefish and permit—though fly tackle has become more and more popular.

Fast-running pelagic (open-water) species such as wahoo, bonito, smaller tuna, amberjack, and sailfish are popular fare with smaller fishing boats. From the Bahamas to the Virgin Islands, Baja to Big Sur, tourists and travelers pay up for a day of "grab bag" open-water trolling. Saltwater anglers on the Pacific troll and boat cast for jack crevalle, dolphin, bonito, and yellowtail, often using light spinning and fly tackle, or a top-quality bait-casting reel. When the ticket prices are higher and the tackle is bigger, the game is bigger; marlin, sailfish, and tuna are the most popular Pacific Coast trophies. Trolling for chinook and coho salmon is highly popular in the Northwest, and most captains will use bait-casting or trolling reels with herring rigs to boat the bright salmon.

The angler choosing saltwater tackle often has less room for error than freshwater fishermen. Ocean fish are larger, and are not caught as frequently. When you've got a hot fish out there, you don't want to lose him. It might be the only catch you make that day. One weak link in a tackle outfit can mean a lost fish. Angling success on the ocean requires that the angler, or the captain advising him, know the specific fishing situations he expects to encounter.

Saltwater initiates should do some legwork before buying any tackle at all. Find answers to these questions:

- What kind of fish will I be trying to catch? How large will they be?
- Where will I be trying to catch them? On the surface? How deep will I need to send my bait or lure?
- What is the geologic formation of the beach, surf, or ocean area where I will be fishing?
- If I'm going in a boat, will I be standing up or sitting down?
- How much sensitivity will I need in my tackle? A stiff, heavy rod to force fish up from the deep? Or can I go lighter? Will I need high-tip sensitivity to feel the fish's soft take? Or will he slam it like a freight train?
- How far, if at all, will I have to cast?
- Will I need special leaders and terminal tackle? Will I be after bluefish or barracuda that can snip through 50-pound mono leaders?

These may sound like difficult questions, but generally they are not. By reading or

Left: *A captain sets the trolling lines. Only by trolling can large baits be propelled at the fast speeds necessary to attract the larger oceanic predators.* **Top:** *The shy but lightning-quick bonefish is the object of desire for many anglers on the tropical tidal flats.* **Above:** *Ferocious bluefish feed nonstop, disgorging food when full while continuing to attack. Schools of bluefish can provide day after day of action for ocean-going charter boats.* **Right:** *The bonito is a fine light-tackle saltwater gamefish.*

© Greg Vaughn/Tom Stack & Associates

The trolling reel is designed with powerful drag mechanisms and well-machined steel gearing to provide cranking leverage against strong and often tireless gamefish.

talking to people who can answer them—tackle shop owners, captains, other fishermen, Fish and Game Commission representatives—the angler can map out what his tackle will be expected to do. With this knowledge the angler will make wise purchases.

Whether using bait-casting, spinning, surf, fly, or boat tackle in freshwater or saltwater, the apprentice angler should understand the correlations between rod size, reel size, line weight, and lure weight. Small rods are designed to cast small lures on light test; larger rods are designed to cast larger lures on heavier test. Light lures cast or troll more efficiently on light lines: since the lures are indeed light, they cannot pull a heavy-pound test line behind them, and any attempt to cast light lures on heavier line will result in short casts that could pull your shoulder out of its socket.

Similarly, heavy lures linked to light-pound test monofilament can snap off when cast, or destroy the balance between rod and lure that promotes "action"—the ability of a

© Allan Weitz

lure to wiggle, move, shake, dart, and swivel in its imitation of a struggling baitfish. Balanced fishing line is strong enough to withstand the pressure of casting and fish fighting, and light enough to pay out and retrieve smoothly and efficiently. Each rod or reel is marked with the lure and line weights it is designed to cast. Lure weights range from $1/16$ of an ounce to 3- or 4-ounce surf-casting plugs or heavy live baits. Fishing line, whether monofilament or braided, ranges in pound test (the amount of weight the dry line can hold without snapping) from 2 pounds for small freshwater fish to 15- and 20-pound test for stripers, blues, dorado, bonito, blackfin tuna, to 50-, 60-, and even 130-pound test for the big meanies of the deep.

Fishing line should not be any lighter than the rod's capacity to absorb and transmit movement on the line to the angler's hand. If the rod cannot "feel" the shaking, vigorous motions of a hooked fish, the fish will likely break off the light line against the stiffness of the rod. One last note of advice on spinning, fresh or saltwater: Always fill your spinning-reel spool up to about $1/16$ of an inch below the flange. A spinning reel holding too much line will not lay evenly, and will tangle easily. An under-filled spinning reel will not cast far—the friction of line against reel and guides, as it pays out, will pull the cast short.

RODS

Whatever rod you choose, look for these construction features that distinguish better rods from cheap-come, cheap-go assembly-line jobs:

- Stainless steel or aluminum-oxide ceramic guides;
- Reel seats should be made of corrosion resistant metal and have screw locks;
- Epoxy, not a varnish coating, on the rod blank;
- Double-wrapped guides.

"Taper" is a popular, but useful buzzword among tackle pros. Fast taper rods have whippier tips and more snap throughout the rod blank (the core tube around which the rod is built), thus they are more responsive to the casting motion. Stiffer rods draw power from the reinforced butt (the "handle" end of the rod) and have slower, softer tip action. Slow taper rods lend the angler more leverage in fighting a fish—and, therefore, allows him to put more pressure on the fish without risking line failure.[1] Always buy the rod with the action that feels right for your hands and "swing" or casting style. A balanced taper rod, however, will provide the most flexibility.

Courtesy Shakespeare

© Jeffrey Sylvester/FPG International

The short and stiff trolling rod is made of re-inforced fiberglass to provide plenty of back-bone. Quality big-game trolling rods will include roller line guides to reduce line friction, corrosion resistant metal reel seats with screw locks, and epoxy coating on the blank.

Bottom Fishing

Ultralight saltwater spinning rods that cast light lures and baits will serve those anglers who choose to bottom fish for Atlantic small surf and inlet fish that include sea robins, porgies, and whiting, or Pacific coast inshore and estuary fish such as corbina, surfperch, and greenling seatrout. Most of these fish are fairly easy fish to catch from the boat or shore, and offer no sport on heavier tackle. Ultralight spinning rods run 6 to 7 feet long, but provide a little more backbone for the more tenacious bottom feeders at 7½ or 8 feet. Line of 6- to 10-pound test is the heaviest the ultralight saltwater sportsman would need, mated with a faster taper rod to provide sensitivity to nibbling.

Jigging and bottom-fishing for saltwater species of moderate-sized fish such as small fluke, cod, halibut, croakers, and tautog, require larger rods running from 7 to 8 feet in length and designed to carry 8- to 12-pound test line. These saltwater rods are generally spinning outfits. Bringing a sluggish fluke to the net requires heavy cranking and hauling, and a very light rod will make this job twice as hard. Still, most inshore bottom fish are fairly small and do not require more than 10-pound test and a light- to medium-weight rod. The stiffness and strength of fiberglass, and its economy, make it the overwhelming choice of most manufacturers of medium and heavy saltwater rods. Bottom fishing for flounder, halibut, and cod requires medium to medium-heavy fiberglass rods with stiff butts and tapers to give the angler good leverage for cranking 20- or 25-pound flatfish from the deep.

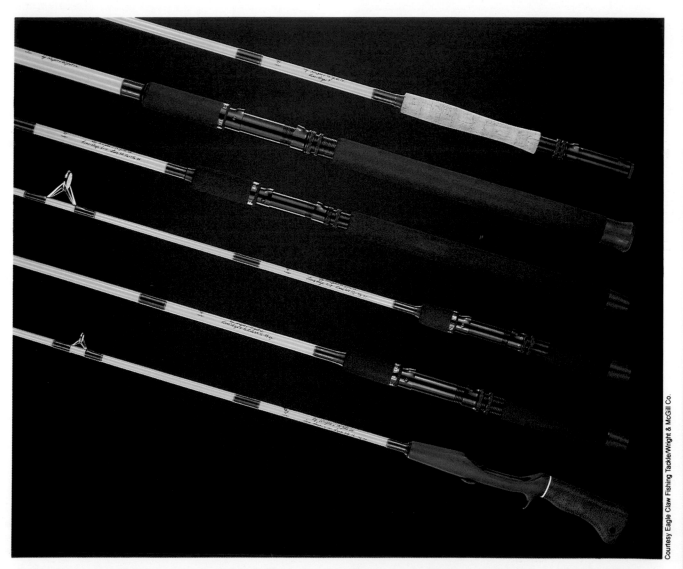

Courtesy Eagle Claw Fishing Tackle/Wright & McGill Co.

Saltwater gamefish are stronger than their freshwater counterparts, and it is crucial that the angler's rod match his or her angling situation if prime specimens are to be landed.

The permit is the fullback of the warm water tidal flats: he won't take the ball much, but he'll absorb a lot of punishment without going down.

Flats Fishing

While commercial-sport tarpon fishermen prefer heavy trolling reels and rods fitted with 20- or 50-pound test and steel leaders to provide novices and one-timers with better odds at landing, or even hooking a bucking tarpon for a few jumps, the sport becomes more interesting at slightly lighter levels of tackle. Many anglers working the tidal and saltwater flats, or mangrove swamps of southern Florida, Belize, Costa Rica, or other Caribbean and Southern Atlantic hot spots, prefer to cast big plugs and jigs, and medium-heavy bait-casting rods of 6 feet or so with stiff tips to help set the hook in the tarpon's armor-plated jaws. Experienced tar-

pon anglers rarely use more than 15-pound test monofilament. Spinning outfits are also common, and, fly-fishing tackle aside, offer the tarpon connoisseur more versatility in casting and a quicker "trigger" for strikes and casting changes, but provide less leverage in setting the hook and fighting the silver-plated tank of the flats. Spinning for tarpon on the flats involves an 8- or 9-foot rod with plenty of butt-power, 10- to 15-pound test, and a medium-sized spinning reel. The tarpon is a thrilling catch, in part because of its spectacular leaps, its sturdy prehistoric body, the quiet tropical setting where it is caught, and because its sheer strength makes it dangerous.

Surf Casting

Surf casters use long spinning and surf-spinning rods from 9 to 12 feet long, designed to hold line in the 12- to 20-pound test range, and designed with long butts for full-body, two-arm casting. Long, fast taper rods with plenty of hip and flex are vital for casting heavy lures beyond the surf to gamefish-rich gulleys and rips. Surf fishermen often prefer a lighter fiberglass-graphite composite rod that is not as fatiguing to cast, since it can take many, many casts over many hours to yield the prize. Where the desired fish differ, so does the equipment.

The surf-spinning reel is mounted below the rod with an open-face spool and a smooth, adjustable star or rear-mounted drag. Spinning reels are very popular with surf casters, and rightly so, because they present fewer backlash and snagging problems on long casts. Adventurous fly-fishermen cast streamers for blues.

The legendary A.J. McClane, in his definitive *Fishing Encyclopedia,* evokes the beauty and the challenge of successful surf casting: "The surf caster must be both hunter and fisherman. Whatever his quarry, it will be necessary for the angler to search for the most promising locations and then take due notice of signs that indicate the presence of feeding gamefish. Tide, wind, weather, and water must be taken into account."[2]

© Anne Duncan/Tom Stack & Associates

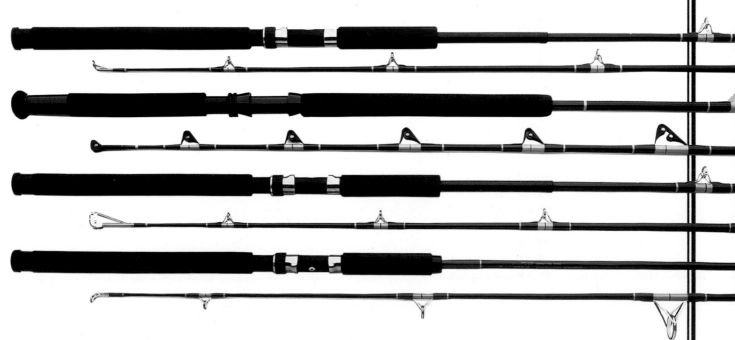

The surf-casting rod is built with a long handle and fast-action taper.

The surf angler must be able to read incoming tides and surf zones like a topographical map. Some gamefish, such as the striped bass, prowl the middle of heavy surf to feed on baitfish suspended in the waves. Many larger predators move into the surf at night, where they can be caught within twenty-five yards of shore.

Big-game Fishing

Big-game fishing makes a dramatic departure from the usual casting and retrieving dialectic of the rod and reel. Hooking and subduing fish such as bluefin tuna, marlin, and shark requires the coordinated powers of the angler, the boat captain, his first mate, and the boat itself. The tackle, from rod to hook, must stand up to the punishment.

Big-game rods and lines—what pros call ''boat tackle''—are usually divided into IGFA certified weight classes: 12-pound, 20-pound, 30-pound, and so on up to 130-pound tackle. The test refers to the strength of the line, but each class of line can be matched to a rod of the right length, flexibility, and weight. Most trolling rods are thick sticks no more than 7 feet and no less than 6 feet in overall length, and are fixed with at least 5 roller guides to cool down wire line friction and resist abrasion. Super-tough tubular fiberglass is the construction material of choice. Most rods are made with chrome-plated reel seats

© Allan Weitz

© Richard Alcorn/FPG International

hooded with locking rings to reinforce the reel against fish-fighting stress.

Trolling reels are classified by the O (for ocean) system, with the lightest reel starting at 2/0 and the heaviest designated as 12/0. The reel numbers roughly correspond to pound test, as the table below demonstrates. "Best Quality" reels are cut from a solid bar of aluminum and fitted with precision-engineered drag systems. The drag function is crucial in fighting pelagic game, both in controlling the first post-strike run of the hooked fish, and in tiring him through the middle and final stages of the battle. Larger reels are fitted with harness lugs on the end plate, which allows the angler in the fighting chair to secure his reel to his shoulder or kidney harness. (Fighting chairs, which allow the Great White Angler to use leg and back power in resisting the mighty run of his enemy, are crucial to successful big-game fishing.)

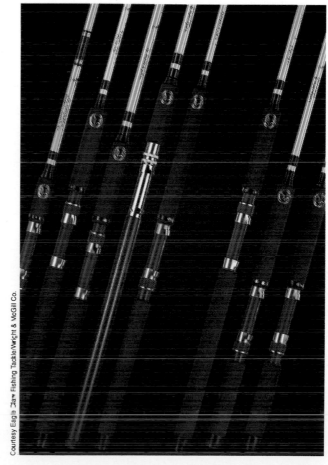

Left: *Without a fighting chair, the angler would have to meet the strength of large gamefish on a wet deck with arm, back, and shoulder muscles.* **Top:** *The moment of truth is at hand.* **Above:** *Sailfish! Setting correct drag is crucial when battling a gamefish in these early, fresh stages of battle.* **Right:** *Wright-McGill saltwater rod models.*

© Allan Weitz

Courtesy Eagle Claw Fishing Tackle/Wright & McGill Co.

A hefty male dolphin of this size can fight the light-tackle angler for over an hour.

© Allan Weitz

Big-game Tackle Specifications

This chart provides generally recommended weights for big-game rods, and correspondences between fish, rod, and reel sizes. This is vital information for the budding high roller who wants to match his tackle to his fishing situation.

LIGHT

Species	Reel Size	Line Test (lbs.)	Rod Weight (oz.)
Atlantic Sailfish	2/0 – 4/0	12 – 20	6 – 9
Pacific Sailfish	2/0 – 4/0	12 – 20	6 – 9
White Marlin	2/0 – 4/0	12 – 20	6 – 9
Striped Marlin	4/0	12 – 20	6 – 9
Blue Marlin	6/0	20 – 50	9 – 16
Black Marlin	6/0	30 – 50	12 – 16
Swordfish	6/0	30 – 50	12 – 16
Bluefin Tuna (Giant)	9/0	16 – 20	16 – 20

MEDIUM

Species	Reel Size	Line Test (lbs.)	Rod Weight (oz.)
Atlantic Sailfish	4/0 – 6/0	20 – 30	9 – 12
Pacific Sailfish	4/0 – 6/0	20 – 30	9 – 12
White Marlin	4/0 – 6/0	20 – 30	9 – 12
Striped Marlin	7/0	30 – 50	9 – 12
Blue Marlin	9/0	50 – 80	16 – 24
Black Marlin	9/0	50 – 80	16 – 24
Swordfish	9/0	50 – 80	16 – 24
Bluefin Tuna (Giant)	9/0	80	16 – 24

HEAVY

Species	Reel Size	Line Test (lbs.)	Rod Weight (oz.)
Atlantic Sailfish	6/0	30 – 50	16 – 18
Pacific Sailfish	6/0	30 – 50	16 – 18
White Marlin	6/0	30 – 50	16 – 18
Striped Marlin	9/0	80	18 – 20
Blue Marlin	12/0	130	24 – 30
Black Marlin	12/0	130	24 – 30
Swordfish	12/0	130	24 – 30
Bluefin Tuna (Giant)	12/0	130	24 – 30

The line measurements are IGFA regulation, which means they will break exactly at the designated weight level.

BAIT CASTING

For those fishermen who largely bottom-fish, jig, or plug-cast (as many do in the saltwater mangroves and flats of Florida for snook, ladyfish, and tarpon, or work the reefs of Pacific coastal areas for dolphin, trevally, and yellowtail), the surgical casting accuracy and heavy-duty gearing of a bait-casting rig will readily perform the job. Saltwater bait-casting rods run from 5½ to 7 feet, with straight or slightly offset butt handles. Bait-casting rods are built for a range of fishing action, from light to heavy, and any good bait-casting reel will have a free spool (the spool disengages from the gears for effective casting), an anti-reverse mechanism (magnetically slows spool reversal, which can create snarls), and a star drag (some cheaper bait-casting reels are built with a non-adjustable drag).

Bait-casting rigs mean accurate casts and still drag to bring home husky bass and light saltwater fare. The three rods on the left are Daiwa Procaster models; the one on the right is by Eagle Claw.

Bait-casting Tackle Specifications

A bait-casting rig that makes efficient and effective use of the angler's casting efforts should be matched up along these correspondences:

Rod length	Line (app.)	Lure weight
5 – 6 foot	250yds/10-pound test	½ – 1 ounce
6 – 7 foot	200yds/20-pound test	1–1½ ounce
6½ – 7 foot	200yds/20-pound test	1½ – 4 ounce

Daiwa's top-of-the-line trolling rod

REELS

The saltwater angler usually faces a smaller range of choices than stream and lake anglers in finding the best reel: It is not so much a matter of personal preference, but of which kind of reel will do the job. For blues and stripers, surf casters will need spinning reels; bottom-fishers choose spinning or bait-casting reels based on the hauling power they will need; flat and other light boat fishermen will choose an outfit based on how they will fish the snook, baracuda, small tuna, trevally, or other smaller gamers; and most of the rest work from boats where the requirements of free-spooling, outrigging, and the size of the piscine quarry demand trolling reels.

One important point must be made: The strength and reliability of the fishing reel is more important in saltwater than in any other form of angling! The size and strength of the fish caught in the salt really beat up on tackle.

Spinning reels differ from bait-casting and trolling reels in one significant feature: the spinning reel's fixed spool does not revolve. As the line is cast, it is pulled off the end of

the spool, and when retrieved, the line is wound onto the spool with a pickup mechanism. Spinning reels virtually eliminate the snags and backlashes that were unavoidable in early bait-casting reels. Modified spinning reels for surf casting are called surf reels, not surprisingly, and are built with wider spools, and star as opposed to rear-mounted drag.

Despite their advantages, spinning reels cannot effectively spool and cast line heavier than 20-pound test. This limitation is an important one in saltwater fishing where a meaty, racy game fish can challenge 20-pound test line. The spinning reel's principle applications are surf casting, skiff fishing on the flats, and jettie fishing—but, as the makers of saltwater spinning reels will tell you, these are large markets indeed.

Saltwater spinning reels cover a narrow range of line weights; the freshwater models are much more versatile. Jettie-bound jig anglers lean to lighter reels; surf fishermen to the beefier sizes. Standard spinners hold 200 yards or so of 6- to 12-pound test, with 10-pound test the popular line of choice. Intermediate reels hold 200 to 250 yards of 12- to

Bait-casting reels can carry bigger quantities of heavy monofilament for large fish. The size and strength of fish caught in the salt really beat up on tackle. Top quality reels are essential to big-game fishing. Small trolling reels are used on the Great Lakes in pursuit of lake trout and salmon, as well as in tidal zones and estuaries.

© Allan Weitz

©Courtesy Daiwa Corporation

15-pound test, and heavies hold 200 to 250 yards of 15- to 20-pound test. The heavier ranges work best for surf casting, where large striped bass and slashing killer blues will challenge the sturdiest rig.

Saltwater Reel Standards of Construction

- Corrosion-resistant stainless steel or anodized aluminum construction;
- Skirted spool to prevent line tangling around the reel shaft;
- Stainless-steel, heavy-gauge reel bail that snaps firmly into position;
- Conveniently adjustable, multi-disc drag (test drag by stripping out lengths of line; it should pay out smoothly);
- Ball-bearing action (the more ball bearings, the better the reel).

Bait-casting reels are far more popular with freshwater fishermen who need the power of a medium-weight bait-casting rod and reel to bring in bass, steelhead, pike, and other muscular fish, but don't need the heavier action of boat tackle, since there aren't too many 75- or 100-pound largemouths or northies around. While trolling reels are cousins of the bait-casting reel, they are not only too large for casting, but fit with drag systems and low gearing ratios that would make plug cranking impossible.

Sturdy bait casters and their lower, more powerful, gear ratios outperform spinners when jigging or plunking for the big-bottom fish. They also serve exceptionally well in over-crowded, plug-casting situations—for instance, casting to snook in over-grown mangrove Florida rivers—where the short distance accuracy of bait-casting tools allows an angler to make dead-eye casts and easily horse his plug out of trouble. Lighter saltwater bait casters typically hold 250 to 275 yards of 15- or 18-pound test, while heavier bottom crankers, such as the Penn 65, will hold 350 yards of 30-pound test.

Few of us own a private boat and trolling rigs to launch our own deep-sea fishing adventures. Those of us who do are probably negotiating a loan with a banker right now. Most anglers who want to catch the big pe-

© Kenneth Garrett/FPG International

Saltwater reels should be built with corrosion-resistant stainless steel, or anodized aluminum. Anglers pursuing smaller game such as bonefish, redfish, perch, puppy drum, or weakfish can get away with using lightweight saltwater spinning reels, which are less tiring and more convenient to use.

lagic game fish go out with a captain, who provides boat tackle, rigs, and bait. Penn, Garcia, and Daiwa are the leading manufacturers of saltwater trolling reels. Still, most of us wonder how we'll afford a rod and reel, much less an inboard-outboard with a flying deck to cruise North America's tidal side streets and blue-water highways—or even afford to rent someone else's. If we buy a saltwater rig, well, it might have to perform shore as well as boat duty. Much of saltwater fishing is tinged with Gatsbyesque images of faded WASP nobility, of wind blown executives and bestselling novelists wearing crinkly smiles as they hoist a tuna aboard, of rich weekend vacationers snagging blues on the shores of Martha's Vineyard, of men from New York meeting trusty guides in hot Caribbean bars to plan expeditions for marlin and dorado. Although pelagic game-fishing was defined in large part by the most robust Midwesterner of them all, Ernest Hemingway, the sea is open to us all, and with a little ingenuity anyone can find their own way to fish its mysteries.

THE TACKLE SHOP

SALTWATER RODS

BEST QUALITY

Sabre Big-Game

High rollers only need apply. The Sabre is considered among the finest big-game rods made. Strictly a boat-tackle, blue-water rod. Machined-aluminum reel seats. Silicon carbide roller guides. This is a rod for movie producers, auto executives, Texas oil men, and Wall Streeters. $220 and up.

Penn Tuna Stick Trolling

This short, powerful, all-business big-fish weapon is built from incredibly powerful fiberglass with precise tapers and short lengths to offer maximum lifting power. At 5 feet 6 inches, with Aftco roller guides and top, machined-aluminum reel seat, cushioned foam fore and butt grips, this rod could boat Moby Dick himself. This will retail between $170 and $200.

Berkley Big Game Series
Casting, Trolling, Spinning

Berkley Big Game rods are available in casting, spinning, or trolling models. The live-bait-casting model offers plenty of tip action to feel nibbles and slow taper to horse 'em up; trolling models are fitted with a butt gimbal to mount on the boat; spinning models are highly sensitive. Berkley made the rods with fiberglass and Fuji graphite reel seats, as well as stainless steel Fuji guides and Aftco roller guides for the trolling model. Not the ultimate quality, but a reasonable and responsible buy for the man or woman who must own their own trolling rod. $70–$85 retail price range.

Ryobi Matercaster MC110
Surf casting

This 11-foot surf-casting rod has an optimum casting weight of 8 ounces. The butt is 68 inches long, and the rod weighs 21 ounces and uses a large bait-casting reel. A big rod for casting hefty baits long distances, this Ryobi demands vigorous physical health.

Penn International II
Bottom-fishing and Trolling

Professionals prefer this everyday, blue-collar rod for party boat, reef, and wreck fishing. This rod will bring up the stubborn customers: Penn's super-tough fiberglass helps the angler put on the pressure, and keep it on, until the beast is on board. Indestructible. Prices start at $200.

Shakespeare Ugly Stik Tiger Rods

Captains and amateurs alike rely on Ugly Stik Tigers to perform under a variety of sea and fishing conditions. In these new models Shakespeare added fast-taper, sensitive-tip action to a super tough rod built with a graphite and glass weave, and a reinforced fighting butt. Tiger rods are available in four different product lines: bait-casting and jigging rods featuring stainless steel-reinforced guides, Fuji aluminum oxide tops, and graphite-reinforced reel seats. Capacities range from 10- to 60-pound test line.

Spinning rods. The handles are wrapped with long foam foregrips and the guides are reinforced. Available in lengths up to 12 feet—for long distance surf casting of lures up to 8 ounces—and smaller rods for jigging and bait fishing.

Downrigger rods. These workhorses feature Fuji Steelite guides and tip top, graphite-reinforced reel seats and epoxy-coated winds for added durability.

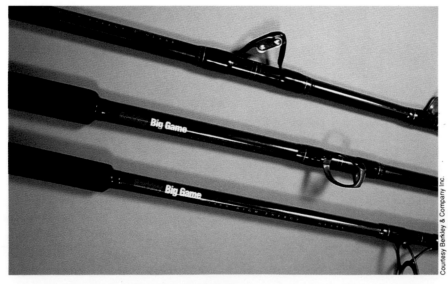

Berkley Big Game Saltwater Series

Courtesy Berkley & Company Inc.

Courtesy Shakespeare

Shakespeare Ugly Stik Tiger Rods

Boat rods. Lightweight construction saves arm and shoulder fatigue, while Aftco roller strippers and tops, reinforced constructions, and twine wrappings above the foregrip protect the blank from heavy-deck plates and gunnel pounding. Prices for these rods range between $65 and $100.

Kunnan Tournament Angler

This superlight 96-percent graphite rod is a boon for the hardworking light-tackle fisherman. The Kunnan saltwater spinning rod comes complete with foam grips, a graphite reel seat, and an extra-strong butt section that picks up the power when a big fish tests the graphite blank. The Kunnan spinning rods are shorter than what many surf casters prefer, running between 6½ feet (for 10- to 20-pound test line) and 7 feet (also for 10- to 20-pound test line) in length and in various models, but they fit shorter jettie, boat, and surf-wading casting situations perfectly. Prices from $60 and up for

models that can handle any denizen of the deep except the largest bills and tuna.

BEST VALUE

Daiwa I.G.F.A. Tournament Series
Trolling

These official big-game IGFA rods, made of a graphite-fiberglass composite, are of interest to the world-record seeker who would like to try a lighter, graphite-composite, fighting chair rod. Available in all IGFA classes from 20-pound test to unlimited. Aftco roller guides, and quality components. A cut or two below the competition in price makes this a tempting buy for the rare angler buying their own boat tackle. From $100 to about $275.

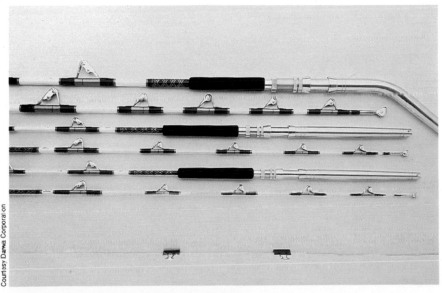

Courtesy Daiwa Corporation

Daiwa Tournament Saltwater Series

Shakespeare Alpha Big Water Rods

Daiwa "Bottom Special" Bottom-Fishing Rod
Bait casting

Dedicated reef, wreck, halibut, grouper, and other big-bottom fishermen of all stripes should welcome this new rod. Reasonably priced, this extra-heavy-action rod relieves the fisherman of much of his labor. Features graphite-composition blank with roller tip and stripper guide, Duracork handle and Daiwa graphite reel seat. The rod is 7 feet long, with a capacity for 50- to 80-pound test line, and it can work baits weighing as much as 2 and 4 pounds! About the weight of the family dog, right? Retail prices begin around $25.

Daiwa Sealine BG Series

Specialty saltwater rods for Florida Keys and Gulf Coast fishermen who cruise the tidal flats, estuaries, and back waters for snook, ladyfish, redfish, tarpon, barracuda, and other warm-water predators.

Back Country: High-content Powermesh graphite, for sensitivity and casting power. This is an ideal light-line rod for Florida back-country fishing. Perfect for bonefish.

Redfish: High-content Powermesh graphite content means casting power and strong backbone.

Spintroll: Graphite/fiberglass Powermesh construction gives the right combination of backbone and tip action for light trolling. Can take the punishment of high-speed strikes and drive the hook home. Fuji stainless-hooded reel seat, Powerlift Grip TM, and tough nylon gimbal with snap over rubber-butt cap.

Jigging: Plenty of power for jigging wrecks and reefs. Prices range from $30 to $40 for all the rods in the series.

Shimano BeastMaster
Spinning and Trolling

Shimano's BeastMasters are built to handle the tough customers of the blue water. Whether trolling, surf casting, fighting the tuna of a lifetime, or cranking a prize halibut from the bottom, the BeastMaster offers incredible backbone and lifting power in all models. Reasonably priced between $45 and $60.

Eagle Claw Starfire Granger Ocean Series

Available in casting, popping, drift-casting, and preeminently in trolling and spinning models. These rods have the muscle to land high stakes saltwater citizens like yellowtail, albacore, and billfish. High quality design includes ceramic tiptops and stripper guides and hard-chromed reel seats that resist corrosion. Good surf-casting rods in the longer models. Excellent rod for the middle-size blue-water fish. Prices range from $35 to $75.

Penn Slammer
Spinning and Bait casting

This all-around saltwater rod suits those who jig, bottom-fish, or troll or boat-cast. This glass/graphite composite rod offers plenty of backbone and hooking-power, but is light enough to cast with all day long. Plenty of additional power and recovery speed for extended fish battles. Corrosion-proof aluminum oxide guides and finish. Priced in the $70 range.

BEST FOR BEGINNERS

Shakespeare Alpha Glass/Graphite 1310 Big Water Series
Spinning

Made of a graphite/fiberglass composite, outfitted with ceramic guides, graphite reel seat and EVA handle, the Alpha is a handsome rod that can take punishment and get the fish in the boat. It's not loaded with a lot of features, and it's made from plain old fiberglass, but in the turbulent conditions

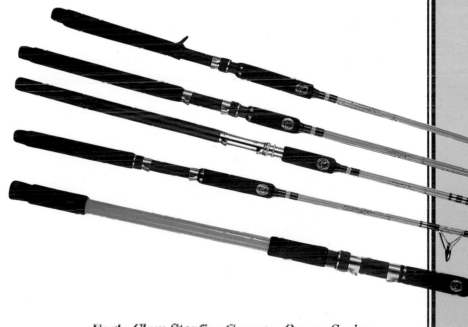

Eagle Claw Starfire Granger Ocean Series

and against big fish of the sea, beginning anglers won't be looking for subtleties. Models are available for bottom-fishing, light boat casting, drifting, or even steelheading, as Shakespeare produces the Alpha in a huge range of model lengths and actions, from a heavy-action one-piecer at 5 feet 9 inches to a 14-foot medium-action surf-casting rod. Between $14 and $18.

Kunnan Competitor
Spinning and Light Surf Casting

This 25-percent graphite/fiberglass composite spinning rod is fitted with EVA foam grips and coated with a durable corrosion-proof finish. A perfectly fine light salt rod for the new angler. Prices between $20 and $25.

Master Striker Rod
Spinning

This is a perfect choice for the younger angler fishing "grab bag," off the local pier or jetty, or the learning surf caster or light-tackle fisherman interested in experimenting with a variety of fish before bearing down. This fiberglass rod is built with yellow and brown wrap, a graphite reel seat, and extended foam foregrips. Two models: A medium-action 8-footer that throws 10- to 30-pound test, and a 9-foot medium-action rod with the same capacity.* From about $25.

*Reel capacity is denoted by pound test/yardage. For example, a reel capacity of 20/500 means the reel will hold 500 yards of 20-pound test line.

TROLLING AND BAIT-CASTING REELS
BEST QUALITY

Daiwa Sealine Tournament Series

This is Daiwa's most expensive reel, designed exclusively for boating huge world-record fish. This is the only big-game tournament reel that can compete in sheer quality with the Penn International. Machined from solid one-piece aluminum, the Tournament has a patented dual-lever drag system, with a locking preset lever to allow adjustments in drag tension in repeatable, gradual steps. Main drag-lever has "positive lockout" to prevent accidental over-setting of drag, which can quickly allow a marlin or tuna to break off the line. Also includes long-life anodizing, positive click control, rod brace, and line index to indicate proper line level. Prices start at over $200.

Penn International

The International is the Mercedes of saltwater trolling reels. Built with the precision of a fine watch, designed to subdue the fiercest and largest of saltwater behemoths, the International is fitted with 120-degree Arc Lever Drag with three set stops for free line, strike position, and full stop. Built with gold anodized aluminum side-plates, the International is made with stainless steel gears only, shielded stainless steel ball bearings, harness lugs, rod braces, and solid-brass rod clamps. This is a triumph of American engineering. Prices start at $225 for the 28-ounce, 12TU Model (carries 850 yards of 12-pound test), and go to more than $600 for the Model 80SW, which carries 1,000 yards of 80-pound test and weighs 118-ounces.

Daiwa Sealine Tournament Reel

Daiwa Sealine Jigging and Trolling Reel

Penn International 30

BEST VALUE

Daiwa Sealine Series

These are cheaper reels in the Sealine series. A high-speed ocean-casting, jigging and trolling reel, cut from a single piece of aluminum, and fitted with stainless steel ball bearings, the Sealine's gear ratio is a racy 5.1 to 1. While not a unilever-drag system—definitely the best—the multi-disc drag provides plenty of stopping power. Anglers putting together their first bread-and-butter outfit for serious boat fishing on the briny should give this medium-priced Sealine serious consideration. Models suit a dizzying array of angling environments. Reel weights range from less than 1 pound to 56 ounces for the largest models. Capacities range from 14/380, 20/280, 25/220 to 50/720, 80/400, and 130/290, with many variations in between. Prices range from $65 to $90.

Penn Senator 113H and 114H

A highly popular big-game trolling reel, the Penn Senator offers quality workmanship with slightly cheaper materials and fewer features than the International. The spool is made of bronze and chrome-plated; the ball bearings are stainless steel. It features star drag and the usual rod clamps and harness lugs for big-game set ups. If the boat you rent has Senators screwed to the rods, you're probably going to have a good trip, catching more fish with less effort. If you buy a Senator and maintain it properly, whether you use it once a summer or every weekend, you will, in all likelihood, be able to pass it on to your children—or your grandchildren. The 113H weighs 34 ounces with a capacity of 30/575; the 114H weighs 52 ounces with a capacity of 50/525. Prices start at a reasonable $60.

Shimano Triton Levelwind

Sturdy, reliable boat-casting and trolling reel at a reasonable price. This graphite reel is very light (14 ounces), and available in two models: Triton "Charter Special" with 4.2 to 1 gear ratio and lever drag, or "Speed Master" with 5.2 to 1 gear ratio and "Fighting Star" drag system. Line capacities begin at 14/300 to 20/330. Prices range from $50 to $75.

Garcia Classic Series

Reliable Swedish craftsmanship with smooth, powerful multi-disk star drag, dual-mechanical and centrifugal-cast control, and a lifetime factory warranty. Push-button free spool and rod clamps are also standard issue with most models, as is a "line out" alarm and self-centering line guides. The more expensive models are built with bronze gears. These beautiful reels are designed with a simple line and primary colors—every part is in the right place for its function. A Garcia belongs in the Museum of Modern Art's permanent gallery of American design! Prices begin at around $50 for the simpler models, and, as features are added, run up to around $80.

Ryobi SL 320 Big Water Levelwind

This all-graphite trolling reel is best suited for medium-weight ocean fishing—blues, stripers, chinook, and dorado. Weighing only 17 ounces, this wonderfully light reel handles 400 yards of 20-pound test and features "Autoclutch" drag, which allows fast engagement from free spool by simply moving the handle forward. The smooth-star drag system won't subdue tuna or marlin, but it'll knock out anybody in the middle-weight classes.

Shimano BeastMaster Trolling

Priced a little under the competition, the BeastMaster is built with two drag settings, two gear speeds, stainless steel gears and 5 stainless steel ball bearings. Weights range from 56.9 to 134 ounces. Prices vary, starting at around $240 and ranging up to $500.

Penn 60 and 65 Bottom-fishing

These workhorses make an excellent buy for those anglers interested in shore, jettie, bridge, and dock fishing—or for working large catfish and sturgeon in freshwater. Really great buy for the easy-come, easy-go saltwater angler. Bite! Penn 60: 30/275 capacity; 19½ ounces with gear ratio of 2.5 to 1. Penn 65: 30/350 capacity 20½ ounces with gear ratio of 2.5 to 1. $20–$25.

SPINNING REELS

BEST QUALITY

Crack 300

Solid, reliable surf-spinning reel, popular with surf casters up and down the East Coast. Gear ratio is 3.3 to 1, and the reel holds 250 yards of 20-pound test line. Prices run around $100.

Orvis Saltwater Spinning Reel, No. 3

Courtesy Zebco Corporation

Quantum QSS Saltwater Rods

Quantum QSS

This is an exciting new model featuring a rack of innovations. Quantum is taking its best shot at the industry leaders in saltwater reels—Penn, Shimano, and Daiwa. The QSS gears are made of high-grade stainless steel, not brass. The QSS drag system features oversized discs that work in tandem with the aluminum spool to form a "heat sink" that dissipates high temperatures. Gears and parts are anodized and protected by SaltGuard anti-corrosion sealant. The rear-mounted BaitSensor switch puts the reel in adjustable free-spool mode for live lining bait, surf fishing, or dropping back off outriggers. Flip the switch right or left and the spool reengages instantly to preset drag tension. The QSS also includes an automatic bail mechanism, right-left conversion, anti-reverse, and many more features. Quantum has made a spinning reel that aims to make a serious run at the competition.

BEST VALUE

Orvis No. 3 Spinning

Matched to a 7- or 8-foot heavy-action rod and a 10- to 15-pound test line, this heavy-duty but light-weight (14 ounces) Orvis spinning reel is perfect for surf casting or tarpon hunting on the flats. Features rear-mounted drag system, high-speed gear ratio (4.6 to 1), and convertible right or left hand wind. Prices start at around $65.

Penn Spinfisher Series
Surf Casting

These handsome spinning reels are fitted with gold anodized corrosion-resistant skirted spool and jet-black housing. A high-performance spinning reel, the Penn Spinfisher features high-speed retrieve in the region of 5.1 to 1 gear ratio in the lighter models, and all models are made with three ball-bearings and silent anti-reverse. The heaviest reel weighs 26 ounces, with a capacity of 20/250, and perhaps the best model for surf casting is the medium-weight saltwater Spinfisher, with a 4.8 to 1 gear ratio, weight of 22 ounces and 15/330 capacity. The lighter models are feasible for fresh and saltwater, with line capacities in 6- and 8-pound test.

Shimano Baitrunner
Surf Casting

These medium-weight spinning reels fit the bill for light saltwater flats and surf fishing. Made of a graphite and titanium composite, with stainless steel bearings and a Baitrunner tension adjuster. In sizes from ultralight to heavy-saltwater, with gear ratios ranging from 5.2 to 1 in the 140/6 capacity reel (13.9 ounces), to 4.2 to 1 in the 230/25 (23.5 ounces) capacity reel—the best surf casting model except when very small blues are running. Prices start at $40.

Freshwater Tackle

Most fishermen see saltwater and freshwater fishing as virtually two separate sports, and are passionately partisan about their preference. Yes, sometimes the trout fisherman may surf cast for blues, or a fluke angler may take his boat and troll a local lake. But most of us grow up fishing in either freshwater or saltwater and, like Democrats and Republicans, we never leave the party. The saltwater fisherman is more like the big-game hunter in Africa, carrying powerful, can't-miss equipment because he might have only one chance to bring down his strong, fast-moving quarry. On the ocean or even from the shore, the saltwater fisherman does not know nearly as well as his freshwater-fishing counterpart where the fish are going to be, and what fish he will find—and he might find a very large fish. Saltwater fish are strong and fast for their size. So he uses equipment heavy enough to handle the extremes.

The freshwater fisherman is more like the uplands small-game hunter, who knows exactly what he is hunting for, where it lives, and what firepower is needed to bring it down. Small-game quarry is more elusive, harder to find, flush, and shoot (while the big-game quarry is easy pickings once you find it). The small-game hunter's edge is his detailed knowledge of the habits and habitats of his quarry. He must carefully approach and track his quarry, and once he has found it, he must shoot with precision.

So it is with most anglers on the streams and lakes of North America. The knowledgeable fish tracker must also have a clear idea about what the fish are biting and when they're feeding actively. The complex environments of small lakes, streams, and rivers make most gamefish—except for those at the very top of the food chain—cautious, shy, and very specific in their feeding patterns and movement. The freshwater fisherman must carry equipment tailored, not only to the fish he wants to catch, but also to where that fish will be found. An entire category of tackle, for instance, has sprung up around fishing "structure"—especially for largemouth bass. Using the right equipment at the right place and depth means more hook-ups.

Freshwater gamefish tend to be stationary (think of trout, bass, muskies) rather than migratory as are many top saltwater species: Precision of delivery counts highly in successful freshwater angling. Unlike tarpon, blues, or tuna, freshwater gamers rarely school, and must be sought out individually.

The variety of freshwater equipment is greater, but its weights are lighter. Freshwater tackle performs four main functions: spinning, bait casting, spin casting, and fly-fishing. But within these main styles exist numerous subcategories. Some companies specifically design large spinning rods to catch steelhead or muskies. Bait-casting reels range from heavy Great Lakes salmon rods to "pitchin' sticks" expressly built for crappie fishing. As a freshwater angler, you may know or will discover that a good tackle outfit will give you plenty of versatility: Freshwater game fish fall into a narrower range of sizes than saltwater species, one class of tackle can handle a fish in a variety of sizes. Fly-fishing is the exception to this rule. Spinning rods and open-faced reels are highly popular. They serve any number of freshwater purposes and are particularly effective in light and ultralight outfits for the pursuit of the smaller, livelier game fish trout and smallmouths. The spinning rod casts farther, quicker, and with fewer snags and foul-ups than bait casters.

Spin-casting rods and reels are also easy casters, but don't match the performance of other tackle. Zebco and other manufacturers have, however, kept themselves in clover by selling spin-casting outfits to young people and raw beginners. Push-button operation makes them very easy to cast and retrieve. Spin-casting reels resist line snarling and cast accurately, but not with great distance. They won't handle large fish very well: taking tarpon with a spin-casting reel is nearly impossible.

Bait-casting rods, of course, use the side-cranking bait-casting reel, which is more difficult to operate than the spinning reel. The bait-casting outfit, however, is the sturdy, muscular workhorse of freshwater tackle. The cranking mechanism and layered star drag provide the angler with more leverage to cast heavier plugs and land stronger, heavier fish. The bait cranking graphite reels of today have gained great popularity among bass fishermen, who rely on their power to horse cantankerous bass out from under cover.

Expensive graphite and boron rods transmit more sensitivity to the angler's hands, while offering the most fiber stiffness (or modulus) at the lightest weight. High-grade fiberglass rods are almost as sensitive as graphite and boron, but cheaper. Still, many anglers feel the weight differences.

© Carl R. Sams II/Dembinsky Photo Assoc.

Courtesy Cabela's

Left: *Brown trout, steelhead, and king salmon: not a bad day's work.* **Below left:** *Freshwater angling is more of a casting and retrieving than a trolling enterprise, which makes the simple, lightweight and easy-to-cast, spinning reel very popular.* **Below:** *A crucial part of an angler's tackle is his patience.*

ULTRALIGHTS

Ultralight rods run 4½ to 5½ feet in length. These super whippy high-strung rods cast lures that weigh as little as ¹/₁₆ of an ounce. Casting range is limited, which makes them ineffective in large bodies of water, save for specific situations where short-distance fishing is possible. Ultralight outfits can make for a spectacular day of sport under the right conditions, but will work for few fishermen as "every day" rods. For the experienced angler, ultralight spinning presents one of the most precise challenges in fishing.

Ultralight spinning means great sport for panfish, smallmouth bass, trout, and other wary game fish in skittish, narrow, low-level streams where banks are high or overgrown. This requires accurate short-distance casting that creates minimum water disturbance. Ultralight spinning rods weigh between 1½ to 2½ ounces, are 4 to 6 feet in length, and will use less than 3-pound test monofilament. So armed, the angler is prepared to stalk small, wily fish in hard to reach places with tackle that leaves no room for error.

The reel and rod must be high quality. Casting wispy lines and small lures requires exceptional response from the rod, and delicate drag settings. As the angler—equipped with an ultralight rod and reel—casts upstream, he controls the line with his finger, drops the cast at an exact location and then pulls his spinner off the shallow bottom and up into the water.[4] When the angler begins retrieving the line, the line displays "action." Taking trout, small bass, or frisky perch on ultralight gear is a delicious challenge that must be tried to be appreciated. A half-pound fish hooked on ultralight tackle offers an unbelievable fight.

LIGHTWEIGHTS

Lightweight rods will suit the eclectic fisherman after a variety of game fish under 2 or 3 pounds. Light rods range in size from 5½ to 7 feet and will accurately cast lures up to a half-ounce in size. Most freshwater spinning reels will fit this rod, but the smaller, lighter reel models will give you a more balanced outfit, which will allow accurate casts of short or long distances and more rod control when you fight the fish. The lightweight tackle class is the best in which to build a bread-and-butter outfit, unless you consistently fish for pike, salmon, or steelhead.

MEDIUM-WEIGHTS

Medium weights run about the same length as lights—5½ to 7 feet—but are manufactured with stiffer butt ends, and less taper, for firmly hooking and playing large fish. Medium weights are also appropriate when fish are small but require more to hook the fish, pull them out of cover, or to cast into brush. This is the tackle class for today's serious game fisherman, whether stalking trout, pike, striped bass, steelhead, small salmon, char, or other grown-ups that weigh from 3 to 5 pounds. However, medium-weight rods, if fitted with light monofilament, will offer good sport for smaller quarry, as well. Medium-weight rods and reels generally offer the angler the most cooperation when line tests are between 8 and 15 pounds.

HEAVYWEIGHTS

Heavyweights range from 6 to 9 feet in length. These large, long-butted rods will only fish comfortably with large spinning reels (not a spin-casting reel), and strong line (8- to 25-pound test). They can handle heavy lures designed for America's strongest, huskiest open freshwater fish.

The beginning angler launching a modest career in his local reservoir, stream, or river, armed with modest ambitions of landing bass, perch, or some nice little speckled trout doesn't need a hawg-bustin' reel or thunderstick rod to jerk 8-pound bass out of cover; nor does he need an expensive Thomas & Thomas spinning outfit, favored by English aristocrats for salmon and trout fishing on their private beats of the Test River. A moderately-priced, lightweight quality spin-casting or spinning outfit will serve well.

SPINNING REELS

The construction features of high-quality spinning reels were reviewed in the saltwater section. While the freshwater reel does not need to be corrosion-proof, it should offer ball-bearing construction, a reliable bail mechanism, smooth running drag, pop-off line spools, silent anti-reverse, and the correct gear ratio for the angler's preferred fishing situation. High-speed reels, designed for high-speed lure and bait retrieve, sport gear ratios of at least 5 or 5½ to 1. Reels geared with ratios of 3 or 4 to 1 give better accounting to slow-retrieve lures, while anything lower is strictly for cattie and carp fishing.

Far Left: *This angler hoists a king salmon from the Kenai River in Alaska.* Left: *The angler's prey may be bass, brown trout, or a profound peace of mind.* Below left: *Light spin-casting tackle and a long dock on a good lake mean exciting fishing.* Bottom: *Small brooks and streams require utmost stealth from the freshwater fly angler.* Below: *The ponds and lakes of North America are the training grounds for learning anglers.*

BAIT-CASTING REELS

Bait-casting reels are the new celebrities in the world of fishing tackle. In one television "fishin' " show after another, professional bass-fishing stars cast and crank with graphite-composite bait-casting reels. It has become the only reel allowed when the bass fishing is serious.

Bait-casting reel "technology" has seen more vital innovation over the past twenty-five years than any other sort of tackle. Early bait-casting reels—inadequate in landing serious fish—were used mostly by children and senior citizens. Lacking the anti-backlash and level-wind technology of today's bait casters, the early models were notorious for creating the dreaded "bird's nest." When the lure or bait was cast, reel, spool, gears, and handle also revolved simultaneously. Once everything was spinning at the same time, it was difficult for the fisherman to apply thumb pressure at just the right time to drop the lure in the water without creating backlash. I remember many fishing evenings from my childhood spent crouched over my bait-casting reel muttering curses as I picked apart bird's nests while

my Dad continued to cast with his fancy spinning reel. (Of course, he would eventually relent and help me untangle the knots.)

When a large fish was engaged on the old bait casters, the double-handled crank would spin as fast as the lunker could strip line off the reel, which was damned fast. Most fishermen burned thumbs, scraped knuckles, and some broke fingers in drawn-out lunker combat.

Swedish tackle manufacturers originated the free-spool casting innovations that changed the destiny of these reels. When only the spool revolved during the cast, backlash became much easier to control. Models began to appear in North America during the late 1950s, and these new bait casters surged in popularity by the early 1960s.

Now, most quality bait-casting reels have a magnetic anti-backlash device that places slight pressure on the spool so the fishing line does not backlash. Many also include a second brake mechanism that enables the angler to apply friction to the spool through a control knob on the reel's palm plate. Level wind mechanisms (the shuttle guide that deposits retrieved line on the spool evenly) and

© G. Schwartz/FPG International

© Dick Dietrich

© Dave Woncarlich/Dembinsky Photo Assoc.

Opposite page: *The remote lakes of the Pacific Northwest offer the adventurous angler opportunities to cast to wild cutthroat and rainbow trout.* **Above:** *Dropping a line in the West Fork of the Black River in the White Mountains of Arizona.* **Left:** *A record northern pike: as fine a specimen as ever will be caught.*

a range of sophisticated star-drag systems give bait casters a distinct edge against stubborn bass and other top game fish.

Still, even with all these improvements, the most sophisticated bait-casting reel is still susceptible to backlash. With timing and practice, however, the bait-casting angler can learn to stop the spool the instant the lure hits the water. Thumb pressure to the spool should be applied at the start of the cast, eased when the lure is in flight, and re-applied with increasing pressure to stop the lure at the target.

When replacing a rod or reel in your bait-casting outfit, remember to check that your new rod or new reel fits your older model. A reel seat that does not firmly hold on the rod can be a disaster. New bait-casting rods are available from top makers like Shakespeare, Ryobi, and Daiwa in graphite and boron, and when you combine one of these models with a graphite reel, you've got an incredibly comfortable fishing outfit that posts little strain on the shoulders after hundreds of casts. Budding bass masters, steelhead junkies, pike and muskie hunters, and anglers seeking major bottom feeders are all well served by the bait-casting reel, which can weigh as little as 4 or 5 ounces and as much as 15 ounces or more.

Lightweights: Rods of 5 to 6½ feet generally feature whippy action for casting light lures and baits in the ¼- to ½-ounce range. Manufacturers design bait-casting rods in the lightest weights specifically for crappie fishing, a hot fishing fad down South.

Medium weights: These stiffer rods with reinforced butts and less taper range from 4½- to 6-feet long but cast lures weighing from ⅜ to ¾ of an ounce. Anglers who often work in crowded conditions—where creeks or rivers are overgrown with low-hanging tree branches and thick bank cover—prefer the shorter rods for more accurate casting. The medium weights can cast heavier lures in a pinch, up to 1½ ounces. Bait casters working in these weights usually work with 7- or 8-pound test line.

Heavyweights: These stiff rods run a little shorter than some medium-weight rods. Stability is the essence here, as these are the rods that give large salmon, steelhead, lake trout, and saltwater gamers like tarpon and snook, the best accounting. They cast the heaviest freshwater lures and baits, from 1

Above: *Plump, fierce-jawed, carmine-streaked: fly-fisherman's dreams are full of rainbows such as these.* Below: *An assortment of trolling and baitcasting reels.* Right: *Casting to deep-water rainbow trout in the Middle Fork Feather River.*

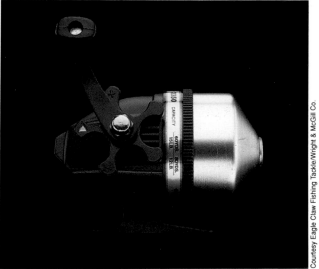

Above: *Even the best spin-casting reels are inappropriate for big-game freshwater fish; these, however, are made of aluminum and graphite and will withstand years on the water.* **Right:** *The angling tradition requires that its skills be taught, one generation to another, binding its fathers and sons together..*

to over 2 ounces. But the angler need not string the reel with line heavier than 15-pound test for any of these fish—unless he lacks confidence in his angling skills.

TROLLING REELS

Trolling reels are the stronger big brothers of the bait-casting reels. The principles of construction are the same, except that the trolling reels are not equipped with the bait-casting reel's numerous ease-of-casting mechanisms.

SPIN-CASTING REELS

Spin-casting tackle is popular with younger anglers. The closed spool and automatic-line-winding mechanism make the spin-casting reel extremely easy to use and cast. The exceptions are the cheap combo kit, some of which are notoriously unreliable. Line is wound around a spool within the closed hood of the reel, and when the line is cast it spools off and pays out through a small opening in the hood. The friction created as the line passes through the hood cuts down on casting distance, especially with smaller lures, which makes spin-casting tackle unpopular with fishermen working large bodies of water. However, the spin-casting reel casts accurately at average distances (provided the line doesn't become snarled around the spool, a common problem).

Spin-casting rods are generally built between 6 and 7 feet in length, and are really modified bait-casting rods. The reel is attached on top of the rod handle as with a bait-casting reel. Large guides and a straight rod handle distinguish the spin-casting rod from its robust cousin.

THE TACKLE SHOP

BAIT-CASTING AND SPINNING RODS

BEST QUALITY

Eagle Claw "Fishin Hole" Graphite Series
Bait casting and Spinning

These one hundred percent graphite rods are available in ultralight and regular, medium, medium-heavy, and medium-light for bait casting and spinning. They feature bonded graphite from butt to tip, high-quality nylon guide wraps, [specie] cork grips, and taper-fit ferrules. The new bait-casting models include crank bait, flippin', and poppin' rod models. The casting rod handles 8- to 15-pound test and ¼- to ½-ounce lures. The flippin' rod carries 8- to 20-pound test, and ½- to 1½-ounce lures and baits, while the popping rod is built to cast 15- to 25-pound test and ½- to 2-ounce lures. This top-of-the-line product ranges in price from $54 to $82 for the heavy popping rods.

Shakespeare Monitor
Bait casting

Track water-surface temperature readings and catch fish at the same time with Shakespeare's new Monitor Rod. A highly accurate, solid-state temperature gauge measures temperature on the surface of the water and gives the reading on a display panel on the rod handle. Great for budding meteorologists and, of course, any fisherman who understands the relationship between the cold or warmth of his fishing hole and how that affects the game fish he wants to catch. The gauge also gives you something to watch when the fish are not biting. This rod is fitted with a "Kwik-Taper" graphite blank for precision casting. Fuji black-on-black aluminum oxide guides reduce line wear.

Fenwick World Class Spinning Series
Spinning

Fenwick's all-graphite construction (including graphite reel seat) means super responsiveness. Fenwick's reputation for quality is well deserved. The WS461 at 4½ feet in length, casting 1⅛-ounce to ¼-ounce lures on 1- to 6 pound test, runs about $85. Longer rods that cast heavier lures on heavier test can cost over $100.

G. Loomis IM6 Steelhead & Salmon Series
Bait casting and Spinning

Among the finest (and most expensive) fiberglass medium- and heavy-weight class rods on the market. Available in steelhead spinning and casting rod, magnum taper "Hot Shot" rods for super sensitivity, and noodle rods for ultralight, ultrasensitive bait drifting. These are fast taper rods built to detect light bites and nibbles and offer the angler a range of power ratings from which to choose, depending on the size of the fish he expects to encounter. These comparatively light rods scale between 5 and 6 ounces, except for the heavier spinning and back-bouncing rods, but no model weighs more than 7 ounces. The shorter rods are 8½ feet in length, the longer models

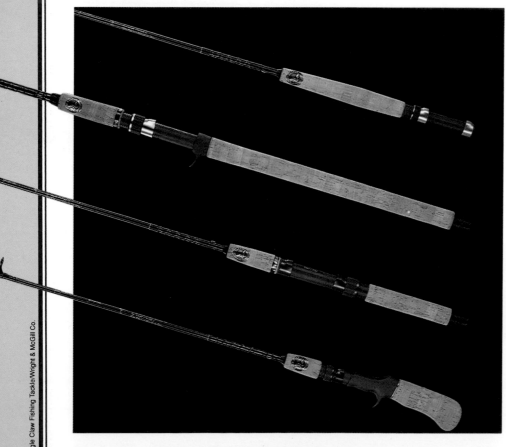

Eagle Claw "Fishin' Hole" Graphite Freshwater Rod Series

Gary Loomis IM6 Spinning and Steelheading Rods

range from 9 feet to the 11½ - foot noodle rods, and 10½-foot ultralight casting rods, which provide maximum steelhead-battling leverage with all possible responsiveness. The situational angler can truly match his tackle to all particular sizes and classes of steelies and their locales with over twenty models from which to choose. Prices start at $200.

IM6 G. Loomis Spinning Rod Series
Spinning

Beautiful fiberglass, ultralight spinning rods. A G. Loomis would be the perfect gift for the ultralight angler, who could then slip into dangerous knee walking, small-spoon casting obsession. These small diame-

ter, fast reacting rods are available in six different models. The 4½ footer can cast lures that weigh as little as $1/32$ of an ounce. The ultralight rods themselves weigh $1^7/16$ ounces and $1¾$ ounces, respectively for the 4½ and 5 footers. Light and medium classes weigh under 4 ounces. From about $100 at your local tackle store.

BEST VALUE

Shimano BeastMaster Fightin' Rod
Bait casting

In fishing tackle, as in other areas of manufacture in recent American history, producers survive and thrive in the marketplace by using technology

to specialize their products. The Shimano BeastMaster Rod is an example of how rapidly this trend is progressing. This rod is not designed simply for a certain weight of fish, or even a certain species of fish, or even a certain species of fish at a certain weight; the BeastMaster is designed to catch big largemouth bass in a particular environment—hard-to-fish structures, weeds, brush piles, sunken logs, and submerged trees and pilings. These robust power rods could yank a horse out of its stable. Reinforced graphite, fitted with pistol-grip handles, and double-wrapped ferrules, the BeastMaster is an instrument of deadly force.

Sizes range from 5½ to 6½ feet in length. For the serious bass fisherman only.

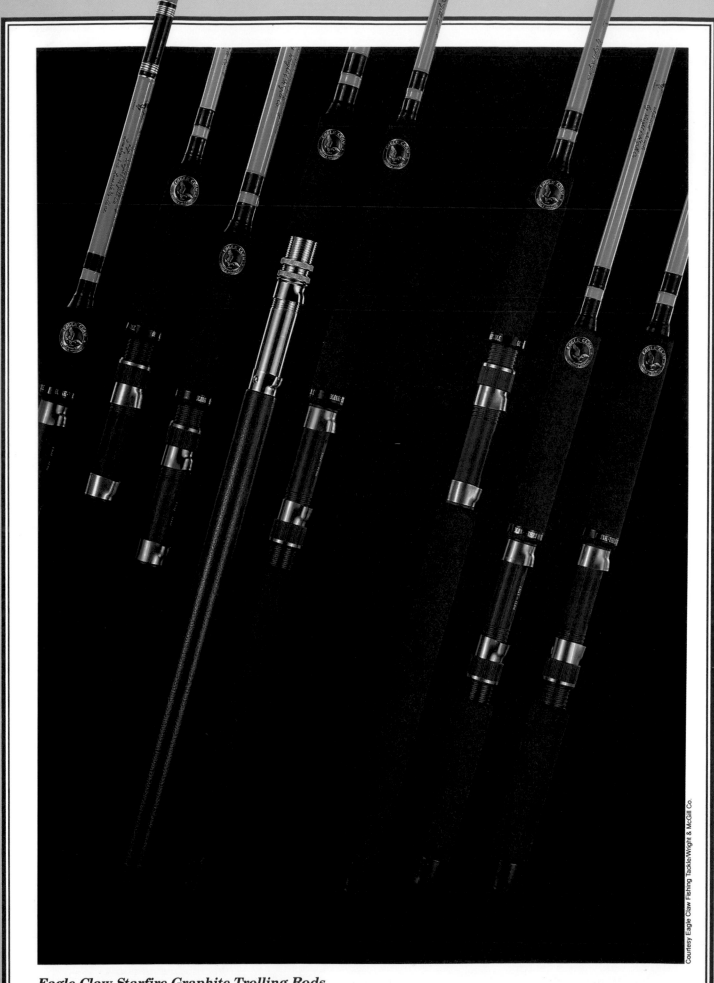

Eagle Claw Starfire Graphite Trolling Rods

Eagle Claw Starfire Graphite Downrigger
Trolling

Eagle Claw's best-bargain, freshwater trolling rods feature ceramic tip-tops, wireframe ceramic guides, and fiberglass taper-fit ferrules. These trolling rods will handle the job for virtually any size salmon, steelhead, or lake trout. From $30 to $73.

Berkley Lightning Series
Spinning and Bait casting

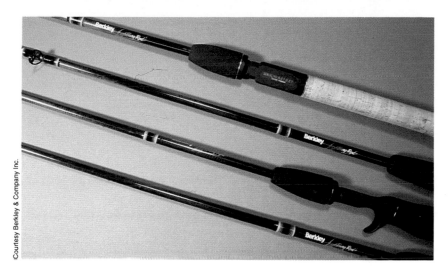

Berkley Lightning Series

Superlight graphite. Most rods in the series weigh less than 4 ounces (the Lightning also comes in bait casting and other freshwater models) and are extremely sensitive, which makes them great for light spinning and very effective on tentative bottom dwellers. The spinning rods cast lures from $^{11}/_{16}$ of an ounce in the smallest 1- to 6-pound test rod, to ½-ounce and ⅝-ounce lures in the longer rods built for 4- to 12-pound and 6- to 17-pound test line. The line features a beautiful ultralight bait caster that throws lures and baits as light as $^1/_{16}$ of an ounce on 2- to 10-pound test line. Capacities run right up to 1¼-ounce lures on 12- to 20-pound test capacities for large bass. Any I.G.F.A. World Record caught on a preregistered Lightning rod wins a $1,000 reward. Prices range from $40 to $50 at retail, though specialty rods will be higher.

Berkley Bionix
Spinning, Bait casting, and Fly

Berkley scientists put on their caps marked "Ultralight" and invented the Bionix freshwater rod series. This one hundred percent graphite rod has been designed to cause as little fatigue as possible for the working fisherman, who makes hundreds of casts over a few hours. At 2.3 and 2.7 ounces, respectively, the Bionix spinning and bait-casting rods are among the lightest on the market. The Bionix is manufactured with "longitudinally oriented" graphite that transmits maximum sensations from the bait or lure—that is, the graphite is layered lengthwise to pass along the smallest vibrations. Bionix means ultralight, ultrasensitive action. Numerous models include a 5-foot-2-inch bait-casting rod that throws ¼- to ⅝-ounce lure weights and carries 8- to 14-pound test; 6-foot bait caster that throws lures between ³/8 and ¾ ounce, and carries between 10- and 25-pound test line. The ultralight spinning reel throws lures as small as $^1/_{16}$ ounce and will efficiently cast 1- to 6-pound test. From $55 at retail—specialty rods in the series will be higher.

Daiwa Sensor Gold Series
Spinning and Bait casting

The light spinning and bait-casting Sensor Gold series features Daiwa's much-lauded, patented Powermesh construction R, and graphite line guides. Excellent middle-priced spinning rods that are especially effective in shallow eastern waters for small fish

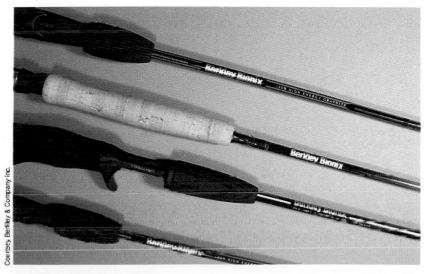

Berkley Bionix Series

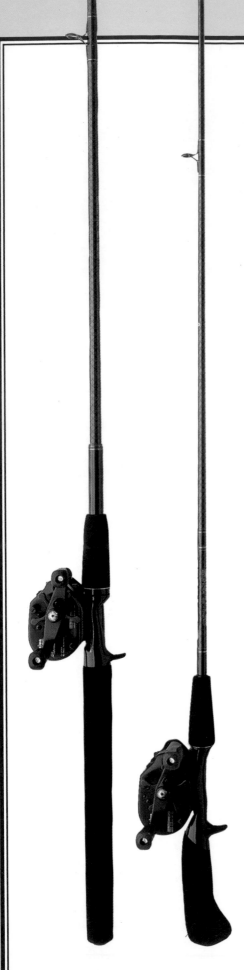

Daiwa Procaster Series

like brook trout and small-mouth bass. The ultralight model is 5½ feet long, carries line between 2- and 4-pound test, and casts ⅛- to ¼-lures. The medium-light spinning rod carries 8- to 12-pound test and casts slightly heavier lures. From about $40.

Daiwa Procaster
Bait casting

Among the most versatile middle-priced rods available. This graphite bait caster is designed with a two-fisted casting handle for greater tip velocity and casting travel. Powerful butts and whippy tips mean strong hook sets and quick, controlled fish landing. Good in saltwater with the heavier models. Available in lengths from 6 to 6½ feet, with the lightest model holding 8- to 16-pound test and casting lures between ¼ to ¾ ounce, up through heavier models carrying 12- to 16-pound test casting ¾- to 1¼-ounce lures and baits or 16- to 40-pound test casting lures that weigh as much as ¾ to 1½ ounces. The Procaster is available in twelve different bait-casting models, including rods with telescoping handles and pistol grips (as opposed to straight handled rods). A variety of top quality models for every situation. Retails from about $55.

Daiwa Muskie Bucktail
Spinning or Casting

This big, heavy-action rod is built with fast taper and tip action to help the angler impart plenty of movement to huge bucktail spinners that draw the reclusive, omnivorous muskie into the open. You can be sure the no-nonsense engineers at Daiwa made sure this rod boasts a stiff butt and backbone, which helps the valiant muskie hunter bear down on the fish, and bring him to the net. This rod is 6 feet ¼ inches long, casts line between 15- and 30-pound test, and lures from ¾ to 2 ounces. You can pick one up for about $25.

BEST FOR THE BEGINNER

Eagle Claw Water Eagle series
Bait casting and Spinning

Eagle Claw's bottom-of-the-line rod still delivers all the performance necessary for the beginning angler. The medium spinning rods run 6 feet in length and handle line weights that range from 2 to 12 pounds. Prices start as low as $14 and you'll pay no more than $35 for the largest rod.

Shakespeare Pro Am
Spinning and Bait casting

Quality and sensitivity at a reasonable price. The fiberglass construction with ceramic inserts, guides, and ferruleless design give the angler good butt-to-tip sensitivity. Sizes run 5½ and 6½ feet and cast 6- to 12-pound test line.

Uncle Buck's Crappie Sticks
Bait casting

A super-lightweight bait caster designed especially for crappie fishermen. These light taper rods detect the lightest panfish strike, and set the hook firmly. From $10.

SPINNING REELS

BEST QUALITY

Daiwa Microcomputer Spinning

This is about as close as you can come to watching a video about fishing while you're out on the water. In their ever-insistent efforts to divorce anglers from their angling common sense, Daiwa has joined other manufacturers in marketing a microcomputer reel. Available in both spinning and bait-casting models, the microcomputer displays retrieve speeds so the angler can duplicate successful retrieves. (Why is it important to retrieve at identical speeds?)

It also beeps at one second intervals to help determine the depth of a sinking lure. (Don't they think fishermen can count?) The spinning model gives the time of day and has a programmable alarm. Graphite made, with a silent antireverse and a 5.1 to 1 retrieve ratio. Weighs 11½ ounces. Starts at about $65 at most retail outlets.

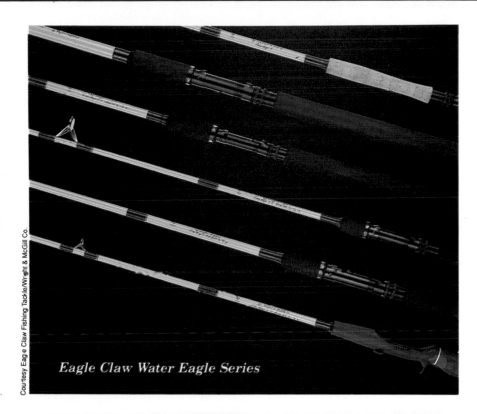

Courtesy Eagle Claw Fishing Tackle/Wright & McGill Co.

Eagle Claw Water Eagle Series

Courtesy Shakespeare

Shakespeare Pro-Am Spinning and Bait-casting Rods

Eagle Claw Gold Eagle

These premium spinning reels feature state-of-the-art construction in models that range from light spinning (7½ ounces) to light saltwater spinning (10½ ounces). The body and spool, among the lightest on the market, are made of graphite. The push-button spool release lets you change spools quickly, and the reel can be fitted for right- or left-hand retrieve. Silent anti-reverse mechanism, rear-mounted drag, folding handle, stainless steel ball bearings and brass-worm gear add up to make the Gold Eagle one of the best available spinning reels of its type.

The models offer these reel capacities: Model 7350 (7½ ounces)—$^4/_{200}$ (which means 200 feet of 4-pound test monofilament), $^6/_{150}$, and $^8/_{130}$; Model 7535 (8 ounces)—$^6/_{230}$, $^8/_{170}$, $^{10}/_{120}$; Model 7540 (10 ounces)—$^8/_{220}$, $^{10}/_{180}$, $^{15}/_{110}$; Model 7550 (10½ ounces)—$^{10}/_{260}$, $^{15}/_{180}$, $^{20}/_{110}$. From $30 to $35 at most retail shops.

Courtesy Eagle Claw Fishing Tackle/Wright & McGill Co.

Eagle Claw Gold Eagle Spinning Reel are available in many sizes.

Shakespeare Whisker Titan Spinning Reel

Shakespeare Whisker Titan and Whisker Titan Lightweight

Shakespeare brings a super-light construction material—titanium—to an innovative new line of spinning reels. The first manufacturer to use whisker titanium in reel construction, Shakespeare calls it "one of the lightest substances known to man." Indeed, the ultralight, 160-yard capacity, Whisker Titan Lightweight weighs in at 5½ ounces as compared to 6 ounces for a Sigma reel of the same size. Titanium is extraordinarily corrosion resistant, and fishermen shopping for saltwater reels should seriously consider any of the Titan's three saltwater models (the lightweight model at 12½ ounces, the medium weight model at 15½ ounces, and the heavyweight model at 27 ounces—about 3 ounces lighter than the heaviest Sigma reel). However, the freshwater fisher-

man who likes a nice outfit, but must pay bills from time to time, might consider whether saving a ½ ounce or so in reel weight makes it worth spending the extra money for the Titan. The Titan is a buy for the very discriminating fisherman. Important features include high speed 5.2 to 1 gear ratio, Teflon-impregnated, ceramic-spool lip that prevents line abrasion; automatic bail closer; and an easy-to-use, spool-applied drag system.

B E S T   V A L U E

Shakespeare Sigma Legend

This is one of the best-selling spinning reels ever made. Models range from the largest saltwater spinning reel on the market (30½ ounces), for sailfish and dolphin on light tackle, to the smallest ultralight reel, (6-ounce ultra-light with four 4 to 1 gear ratio) for panfish or brook trout. Features of the ever-popular Sigma include a surge-free, multi-disc system, die-cast metal gears, high-strength frame and spool of anodized aluminum, securely mounted stainless steel shaft, left and right retrieve, free-turning line roller with Teflon bushing, and a stainless steel, fold-down bail.

Abu Garcia Cardinal 4

A tough, durable reel, the Cardinal 4 is graphite and metal constructed with graphite-reinforced brake discs that quickly dissipate heat and prevent burn-out when a big fish is burning line off the reel. Stainless steel ball bearings, precision-cut, stainless steel worm-gear, and a brass main gear give this reel staying

power and corrosion resistance. Aluminum oxide line roller protects line against wear and abrasion. Abu Garcia guarantees its reels for five years, and this model won't have a hard time making the cut. Line capacities range in four models from ⁴/300 to ¹²/230. Prices begin around $32 and top out around $40.

Quantum QG Pro

Graphite-composite build, with rear-mounted drag system, and silent anti-reverse. The lightest model weighs 6.7 ounces, and carries 120 yards of 4-pound test. The heavy models can be used in saltwater, carrying 275 yards of 20-pound test.

This is a reliable low-priced reel with prices beginning at under $25.

Daiwa Gold Long Cast

Daiwa introduced a new feature on its 1988 spinning reels: a longer, shallower spool to reduce line friction and allow longer casts. The drag system is extremely well-built and adjustable to very fine tolerances. The four models bear line capacities that range from ⁴/145 to ¹⁴/170. All priced at around $50.

BEST FOR BEGINNERS

Mitchell 300 Series

Mitchell has sold millions of these small, solid reels over the past thirty years. Includes all the basic features the spinning angler needs, at a very reasonable price. The reel's all-metal construction means it weighs more for its size than much of its competition, but anyone

Daiwa Gold Long Cast Spinning Series

Eagle Spinning Reel

Daiwa Goldcast Spin-casting Reel

with an arm and a shoulder shouldn't have too much trouble lifting or using the reel. The 300A model costs about $20 with most of the other model prices kept under $30.

Browning 500 Series Graphite

Here's a great price for a quality, lightweight (6½ ounce) graphite reel. The reel does include one ball bearing on the drive shaft, for long-lasting, high-performance retrieve, and strong, dependable rear drag. The 800 series reel has three internal ball bearings instead of one. Retail prices will range between $20 and $30.

SPIN-CASTING REELS

BEST QUALITY

Zebco Classic 33

The distinctive feature of Zebco's popular spin caster is the "FeatherTouch" button, which allows the angler to precisely control the length of his cast. Built with stainless steel ball bearings, cut brass helical gears, and a positive "can't miss" line pickup system. In the $20 range.

Daiwa Goldcast III

Daiwa pushes the edge of the technology envelope in spin-casting reel design. If this reel had any more special features, it'd be a jet. The reel includes an oscillating spool, revolving line pickup pin, multi-disc drag, on and off antireverse, and an oversize stainless steel line guide. Around $30.

BEST VALUE

Eagle Claw Double Eagle Spin Casting

Graphite body and frame. The reel features an adjustable star drag and automatic, silent autoreverse. Many spin-casting reels begin to fall apart after a few short years of fishing—they are notorious for poor workmanship—but the Eagle Claw offers reliable, long-lasting construction. From $18.

Johnson Country Mile Spin Casting

Highly reliable spin-casting reels available in four sizes for the spinner fisherman who doesn't like the look of a spool. Features include an antistatic rotor that pulls static electricity from the nylon monofilament, a "Drive Train drag system", and a free-flow, Teflon-coated line guide. Priced from around $14.

BAIT-CASTING REELS

BEST QUALITY

Daiwa 47LC Levelwind

Here is a top-quality lightweight trolling and bait-casting reel for lake trout and salmon boat-fishing in the Great Lakes and other big waters. The singular feature of this highly innovative reel is the mechanical line counter mounted on top of the reel. This reveals the amount of line that has been cast or released, enabling a precise setting for trolling patterns. A truly helpful device for the less-experienced trolling angler. Retails around $65.

Ryobi E1

The E1 "Computer Control System" built into this new Ryobi bait-casting reel brings fishing tackle into the age of high technology—where some may feel it does not belong. Still, some bait casters will take any measure to control backlash. For them, Ryobi has gone where no reel manufacturer has gone before. The E1 reel features computer circuitry with a lightweight, rechargeable battery pack. The computer provides automatic, magnetic braking only when the spool is about to overrun; the rest of the time, the reel's spool revolves freely allowing longer casts.

The E1 weighs 11.3 ounces, has line capacity of 160 feet of 10-pound test or 140 feet of 12-pound test, features a modestly-fast gear ratio of 5 to 1. This reel is, of course, outfitted with the latest technological innovations in reel design. These include four shielded, stainless steel ball bearings, Handle Drag system, flipping

Daiwa 47LC Levelwind Lightweight Trolling and Bait-casting Reel

switch, and a lightweight graphite and titanium construction. We can next expect to see PC data bases mounted on bass boats that will perform most of the thinking for the fisherman—now that computers can do the casting. Very expensive—about $85.

Penn 2000

This fancy piece of machinery offers two cranking speeds. The hawg buster reels his spinner bait on a 6 to 1 gear ratio—very fast—but, when he gets a strike, the reel instantly shifts down to the much more powerful 2 to 1 ratio. The reel can be custom tuned to shift at different pressure points through a "Speed Shifter" knob located beside the drag. The reel shifts automatically upon strike. Made from graphite, the 2000 offers an array of exotic features, from magnetic casting control to a flipping switch. This reel costs around $70.

Shimano Bantam Fightin' Star

Shimano designed these reels with one overriding purpose: to give fishermen the opportunity to set the most precise drag setting possible. Their "Fightin' Star" drag combines character-

istics of lever drag and star drag to provide the best drag range for line test. The "Strike" drag setting—that is, the setting you prefer when fighting a fish—is established by pulling line off the spool and adjusting the star drag until the tension feel is optimal. When Strike is selected, the appropriate minimum and maximum drag settings are locked in. While the fisherman can adjust his drag during a fight with a fish, he can return instantly to his optimal drag setting. For anyone but the most experienced fisherman, the drag system on the Bantam is really nothing but a useless gadget that will very seldom make the difference in whether or not a fish is caught. Prices run between $60 and $70.

B E S T   V A L U E

Shakespeare Sigma Mag-Lite

This is a competitively-priced lightweight reel that will hold up under years of casting spinner baits, pork rind tipped jigs, worms, crayfish, and fat-lipped plugs. The Mag-Lite boasts the features that the bass boat crowd has come to expect in the bait-casting reels: The reel features an easy to find clicker

Quantum 381 Crankin' Reel

flipping switch; on and off anti-reverse switch that allows the fisherman to lock down the drag on big fish and play out the line by reeling backward; easy spool release; graphite construction, and a magnetic braking system to cut down on snarls and overcasts.

Daiwa Procaster

New from Daiwa, the Procaster offers a blistering retrieve and lots of cranking power with the 7.1 to 1 retrieve ratio. The reel also includes a flipping selector. Magforce anti-backlash control, a power handle, auto-cast with a new lifetime clutch design, and one-piece aluminum frame. The line capacity is 175 feet for 10-pound test line. Prices start at around $50.

Quantum 381 Crankin' Reel

This is a high-leverage, powerful retrieve ratio (3.8 to 1) reel for casting and working crankbaits. Anti-reverse and bushing-bearing construction. This is an excellent reel for the committed plug fisherman. The 381 weighs 8.4 ounces, and carries 125 yards of 12-pound test. About $50 at your local tackle shop.

Abu Garcia Ambassadeur Lite

Machined of a graphite composite, the Ambassadeur Lite

Daiwa Procaster Bait-casting Reel

does weigh in under much of the competition and offers standard and some innovative features for casting ease. The "Lite" weighs 6.8 ounces, and will hold 100 yards of 12-pound test; the "Lite Plus" weighs 7.9 ounces, and offers more gadgets. Both models are built to crank baits at high-speed with a retrieve ratio of 5.1 to 1. Bearings are made of graphite and the gears are made of bronze. The "Lite Plus" offers magnetic spool control, and a flipping switch not offered with the significantly lighter, and cheaper, basic model. The "Lite" will price out around $32 to $35, while the "Plus" will go a few dollars higher.

Abu Garcia Ambassadeur 4600 CB

Designed to handle bigger fish, this Abu is handsomely designed, featuring the Fast Cast ThumBar, level wind, anti-backlash breakers, and star drag. Weighs 9.5 ounces with 120 yard capacity of 14-pound test. Good pike and muskie reel. From $50.

BEST FOR BEGINNERS

Shakespeare Pro Am

This simple bait caster will serve the needs of just about any bait-casting fisherman, short of those entering high-

stakes bass tournaments, or starting their own fishing show on cable television. This reel certainly offers everything the budding destroyer of walleyes needs: an anti-reverse mechanism, solid construction, a spool release, and a line guide. The reel will get the pork rind where you want it—the rest is waiting, and knowing when to set the hook. Good buy.

Mitchell Turbo Mag

Reliable construction with ball-bearing drive and graphite-palming side plate. Gear ratio is 4.8 to 1, and both models in the series weigh 7.8 ounces. About $35.

Courtesy Shakespeare

Lightweight Pro-Am Spinning Reels

On The Lines and Leaders

All freshwater and saltwater anglers, except for fly casters, use braided or monofilament line. The production values essential to quality line are the same for both, though, of course, saltwater fishing generally demands heavier monofilament, which is often linked to steel or wire leaders. Even experienced fishermen may know little about their line except that it is reasonably priced, and only breaks off when a lure is snagged or a fish "they never would have netted anyway" tangles the line, or simply snaps it off. It is important to understand what makes good mono, for good mono is far and away the best type of line for the freshwater or light-saltwater fisherman. It is inexpensive, durable, resists abrasion, and casts far and accurately, thanks to its superior limpness and flex.

Most sportfishing in fresh and saltwater is done with monofilament line; braided line is only used when fishing for large, pelagic fish with trolling rigs. Braided line means big fish. Braided fibers aren't as stretchy and flexible as monofilament. They are wider in diameter and are subject to more wind resistance in casting, though one rarely casts braided line. Their low-stretch values make them attractive to big-game fishermen. The initial shock and powerful runs of a big-game fish make it imperative that the angler have as much leverage as possible against the fish's strength. Stretchy monofilament "gives" too much to the fish's surge, and reduces the angler's leverage.[6]

Look through the promotional copy from line manufacturers, and you will see a small number of different line categories: monofilament, braided, lead core, and wire. Monofilament has much higher abrasion and shock resistance compared to woven multi-strand lines, where each fine strand is vulnerable to wear and tear. But braided lines are woven thick for strength, and boast lower density, which can be important when trolling.

Over one hundred different kinds of plastic resins are blended in various combinations to produce monofilament line, which leads to marked differences in line-field qualities of different manufacturers. Manufacturers, tackle pros, and veteran fishermen judge field line performance by a set group of characteristics. Let's review them here in a quick seminar on the science of fishing line manufacture.

Breaking strength is usually understood as **test strength,** which is the guaranteed amount of dry weight the line can hold before breaking. The strength of the line is virtually always ten to thirty percent higher

Stretchy, high-strength monofilament fishing line in the 15- to 30-pound test range makes saltwater fishing for bonito and other smaller pelagic gamefish an electrifying challenge. Lead core line is used for trolling in deeper water levels.

than the listed weight "test"—But remember that monofilament loses around ten percent of its weight strength when wet! Two different lines can guarantee the same breaking strength, but can have different diameters. And even the tiniest difference in a line's diameter can affect the feel of a cast for the veteran angler.

While many manufacturers don't list this specification, **line diameter** is intimately related to monofilament performance, even in differences of a thousandth of an inch. Line diameter affects spool capacity and wind resistance, which, in turn, affect how far and how accurate the cast, the water drag on the line (which affects trolling depth), the knotting strength and size, and the line visibility. Granted, the average angler may have a hard time noticing these distinctions, but tests do bear out the contrasts in performance. So do your best to compare diameters of the same weight-test lines, and when you can buy finer diameter, do it. Denser lines pack a little more punch when the hook is set in the unfortunate jaws of your victim. The tiniest advantages in tough fishing situations can make the difference between catching a fish or not.

The **density** of fishing line is linked to the diameter: the thinner the line for a particular breaking strength, the denser it must be. The higher the density of the line, the smaller the diameter, and so the faster a line will sink in water and the easier it will cut through wind.[7] Captains interested in deep, thermocline trolling for salmon, lake trout, swordfish, or other pelagic fish equip themselves with high-density line that easily cuts through water.

The **color** of line can provide distinct angling advantages. Seeing the line is crucial to casting and retrieving with precision, and color makes that easier. Bright-blue lines are easy for the angler to follow and less intrusive in the fish's environment. Some monofilaments come in flourescent colors, which are easier to track in darker waters, and can be seen from 40 or 50 feet away in clear water. In bright, shimmering waters, or waters set against a white sandy bottom, dark-colored lines are easier to track.

Courtesy Cabela's

Tying good knots is crucial to the strength and reliability of monofilament. Poor knots diminish breaking strength, and wear on the line.

© Frank S. Balthis

© Arthur Tilley/FPG International

Surf casters generally favor flexible, high-strength monofilament that can withstand abrasion and carry heavy lures for maximum distance without danger of snapping.

Elasticity, strictly defined, is the percentage of stretch a monofilament or braided line will allow before breaking. The stretchier the line, the easier it is to cast accurately, store on the reel, and manipulate in the water. Up to a point. If your monofilament is too "limp"—the word most anglers and manufacturers use to describe elasticity—it will snarl easily during the cast, and make strikes harder to detect. Light pound test monofilament is extremely limp, which can make the soft strikes of walleye or bottom-feeding trout virtually impossible to detect. Nylon is the stretchiest line material, but all of the good, nylon-line makes have been pre-stretched and heat-treated to limit stretch below fifteen percent, with twenty percent the acceptable limit.[8] Many bass anglers prefer a fairly limp mono that will stretch and provide a margin of error when they hook up a hawg that runs for structure.

Shock resistance is the ability of the fishing line to withstand the sudden impact of force, usually in the form of a strike by a large fish. Saltwater fishermen use "shock leaders" to protect the line against the initial strike of a big fish. Braided line offers less resistance to shock than monofilament—but pound test is usually so high that it wouldn't snap if a Great White hit the bait.

Abrasion resistance measures a line's ability to withstand rubbing, scraping, chafing, and grinding against fish teeth, scales, rocks, coral, pilings, river structure, and other natural and man-made underwater obstructions. Of course, deep-sea wire and lead-core lines can tolerate a good deal of abrasion without failure. Braided line, however, is vulnerable to abrasion.[9]

Durability is defined as a line's life expectancy, as guaranteed by the manufacturer and as understood by the angler's common sense and experience. Most fishermen change their fishing line every season. Wire lines are very durable, but are subject to water corrosion. Nylon monofilament will last a long time if it is kept out of direct sunlight and away from heat. Store the line and fishing tackle in dark, cool places—a garage is often the best choice. To preserve the fishing life of your line, always cut back your battered ends, uses swivels when fishing with plugs and spinners, and straighten out monofilament when it bunches up in loops and knots above the reel.

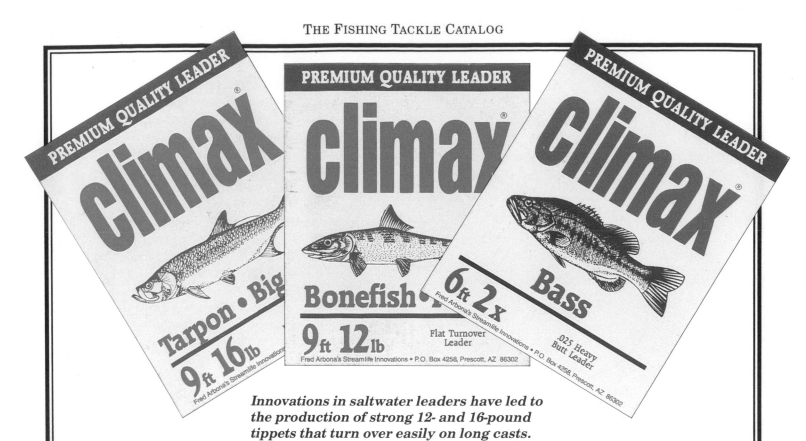

Innovations in saltwater leaders have led to the production of strong 12- and 16-pound tippets that turn over easily on long casts.

SALTWATER LEADERS

The leader splices together the main fishing line and the hook, lure, or bait presented to the fish. In the past, leaders have been spun from silk, catgut, and other materials, but today, all leaders are made of monofilament or nylon-coated stainless steel. Leaders are essential for fly-fishing and trolling. (See Chapter 0 for a discussion on fly-fishing leaders.) Leaders obviate anglers' anxieties whenever the main fishing line might fail at the point where the fish is caught. This can happen for a number of reasons: Too weak— leaders strengthen the terminal rig; too strong—leaders add limpness to heavy test or lead-core line; too visible—leaders disguise dark or otherwise visible fishing line; or too stiff—leaders allow lines, lures, and baits more lifelike and natural action.

Saltwater leaders are made of wire or, more commonly, of nylon. Monofilament offers the angler the most important qualities in leader performance: variety and flexibility. Monofilament leaders are available in all colors, all pound tests, and various stiffnesses. They are resistant to abrasion, durable, easy to handle (most of the time), and are not prone to "shock failure."

Stainless steel wire leaders are very difficult to handle, and dangerous to the hands: use them only when trolling for exceptionally toothy fish. Most boat captains and anglers, surf casters, and other saltwater people favor nylon-coated stainless steel wire leaders, though some like braided wire for its ease of handling and flexibility. Trolling offers full-employment opportunities for leaders of all kinds. The complexity of turning plastic lures and dead bait fish into "living", swimming attractor baits requires as much flexibility as possible in the terminal rig. Heavy lures won't do much shakin' and movin' if they're tied to 75-pound test braided line. Let's review some of the favorite leader choices for trolling and other saltwater fishing situations.

Bite Leaders

These short, heavy leaders (6 inches to 2 feet) protect fishing line from the sharp teeth of tough customers. Single-strand wire, heavy monofilament, or multi-strand monofilament are the materials trolling pros and experienced fishermen use. Some freshwater fishermen use bite leaders when pursuing pike, muskies, or larger walleye. Many pike anglers prefer monofilament, since its limpness and stretch allow the fisherman to transmit much more action to the lure or bait. In freshwater spinning, a short mono leader is advisable for heavier-test fishing line that deadens lure action.

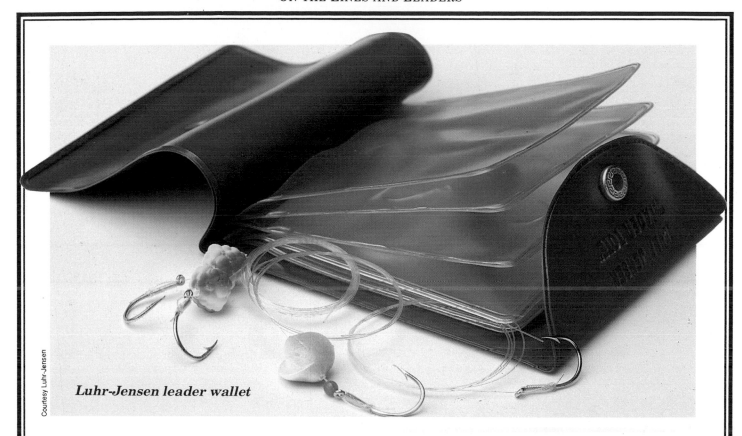

Courtesy Luhr-Jensen

Luhr-Jensen leader wallet

Shock Leaders

The saltwater fisherman often runs into situations where terminal tackle is subjected to a sudden load of stress. Here, an extra measure of protection is needed, since the fishing line is designed to match the weight and sport of the fish the angler's trying to catch, not necessarily the most extreme instances of heavy line stress.

Shock leaders cushion line and terminal tackle against a variety of stress points, from the sudden weight of a large fish striking the bait or lure and leaping or snapping his head, to the jumps and lunges of the hooked fish brought to the gaff. Or, from the sudden strain of the quarry slipping off the gaff and lowering its full weight on the rig, to the hauling up of a thrashing fish without gaff or net.[11]

Often, the trolling angler will make a shock leader by splicing a wire leader to his main line, then splicing a piece of monofilament shock leader to the hook or lure. Monofilament is the only material to bother with in making shock leaders. Since the purpose of the shock leader is to absorb a sudden stress, it only makes sense to tie on the stretchiest line available—and that's monofilament. Trolling shock leaders can run from 3 to 5 feet or more in length, and should at least double the pound test of the line. Surf

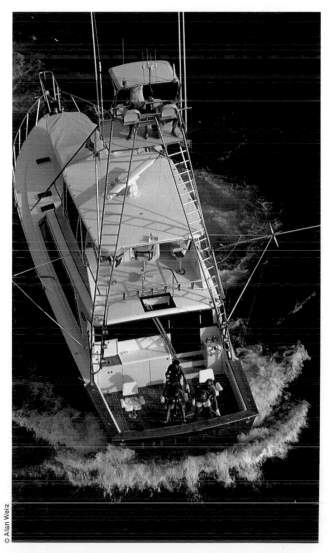

© Alan Weiz

casters will often use long, heavy shock monofilament leaders (about 7 to 10 feet long) to absorb the heavy-line load created when heavy lures and baits are cast long distances—beyond the surf—to running blues or striper holes.

Trolling and Snubber Leaders

When deep trolling lures and rigs in the blue water or the Great Lakes, outrigging anglers need long leaders to stabilize their rig, and allow the lure or bait to offer its most natural action to trailing fish. And when I say long, I mean 50 to 100 feet long. The rig begins at the wire trolling line, which is tied to a swivel and linked to a 50 foot or more monofilament leader. The leader is often swiveled to a herring dodger or flasher, and then crimped to a short, wire bite leader, that holds another swivel, a snelled hook and bait, or a deep-running lure.

Big-game trollers often use what is called a "snubber," a length of latex tubing that encases a doubled-up length of line. When the fish hits the bait, the latex tubing absorbs the hit; if the strike explodes the tubing, the line unfolds to absorb further shock.[12]

Wire "bite" leaders vary in length and test, but their purpose is the same: to keep sharp-toothed gamefish, from pike to bluefish to shark, on line. Berkley is a leading manufacturer.

THE TACKLE SHOP

SALTWATER LINES

BEST QUALITY

Cortland IGFA Black Mono

Ideal for the saltwater big-game fisherman looking to rig up their trollers and tank reels with monofilament instead of dacron. This line can make the kill. Prices begin around $35 for an 800-yard spool.

Ande

Among east coast saltwater fishermen, regular-grade pink Ande is far and away the most popular fishing line used in surf and boat fishing for fluke, stripers, blues, weakfish, bonito, and tuna. Prices range from $8 to $16 for various tests and spool capacities. Double the price for tournament-grade.

BEST VALUE

Sigma Big Water

Designed for super abrasion resistance, this new monofilament for surf casting and heavy saltwater fishing is coated with a super-sleek finish to allow the line to harmlessly slip over rough edges. This also creates a streamline effect which helps casting distance. The line offers strike-absorbing shock strength, and the smaller diameter allows anglers to wrap more footage on a reel spool. Controlled elongation makes Sigma knots more secure under the pressure of fighting fish. Available in weights that run from 6-pound to 130-pound test. Shakespeare lives up to its fine reputation with this new product.

Gudebrod GT Dacron Trolling Line

Braided Dacron coated with DuPont teflon to produce slick, friction-free trolling and re-

Courtesy Shakespeare

Shakespeare Sigma Big Water Monofilament

trieving. The Teflon coating reduces friction between line and guides, and provides extra durability. This is top-quality line favored by professionals and captains everywhere. Around $8 or $9 for 200 yards of 12-pound test line, and over $20 for 400 yards of 20-, 30-, 40-, or stronger-pound test.

Berkley Trilene Big Game

This version of the popular Trilene is designed to withstand the rigors of all-out big-game saltwater fishing, and is designed with a super-hard surface for extra durability, abrasion resistance, and toughness. This line is meant to survive anything. Berkley offers $1,000 to any angler who brings in a world record catch on Berkley Big Game Trilene. Prices start at around $7 for smaller spools and graduate up to around $60 for 3-pound economy fillers.

Cortland Micron IGFA Trolling Line

This is for the big fellas. Heavy braided line of exceptional durability, available in all IGFA classes from 8 to 130 pounds. Prices begin at around $23 for a 600-yard spool.

Mason Silver Lus Trolling Wire

Kink resistant, deep-sinking. 1,000 feet of 25-pound test costs about $20; 45-pound test about $35, and 60-pound test about $50, in 1,000-foot spools.

FRESH AND SALTWATER LINES

B E S T Q U A L I T Y

DuPont Prime

Generally considered the highest quality fishing line by most veteran anglers—and with good reason. Prime (and DuPont Stren) test higher than most brands in knot strength, stretch, tensile resistance, shock resistance, and durability. Prime features what DuPont calls "confilament" structure: DuPont takes a low-stretch, high-sensitivity polyester core and adds a sheath of powerful, shock-absorbing nylon. This offers a combination of suppleness (for casting smoothness and distance) and toughness (for long-lasting

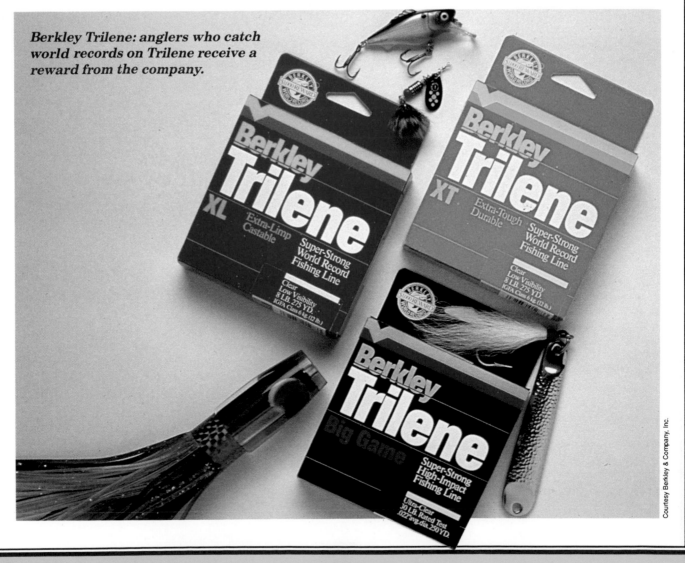

Berkley Trilene: anglers who catch world records on Trilene receive a reward from the company.

wear and reliability in holding a hooked fish). Prices range from $6 to $10 for a 250-yard spool of this quality line.

DuPont Magnathin

A new product from DuPont, Magnathin line provides greater strength at smaller diameters, and smaller diameters mean greater lengths in casting, increased lure depth and action—all of which means more strikes. DuPont claims that Magnithin is up to fifteen-percent-thinner-per-pound test than other leading monofilaments. For longer casting, better lure action, and for near invisibility in clear water, Magnithin can't be beat. In sizes from 2- to 130-pound test.

Berkley TriMax

The highly competitive Berkley company does DuPont's Prime one better by blending three fully "complementary polymer line components." Each separate plastic integrates with the other in the manner of interlocking building blocks, and this provides a combination of line strength, power, and casting distance. TriMax prices run from $8 to $10 for a 275-yard spool, up to 20-pound test.

BEST VALUE

Berkley Trilene XL

If you're looking for super-limp monofilament that resists coiling, you can't do much better than Berkley Trilene. This is the best-selling, premium fishing line in America. Berkley claims that Trilene XL has tested up to twenty percent stronger in comparison tests, but whether you believe that or not, there is no denying the Trilene reputation among most sports fishermen and fishing

professionals, most of whom use Trilene. Trilene XT offers more durability and abrasion resistance. This line compares very well to other premium brands in stretch and abrasion resistance. Prices fall between $5 and $8 for a 300-yard spool, depending on test weight.

Plion II

For extra toughness and effortless casting. Packs abrasion resistance into a surface texture that wears like iron with wonderfully smooth castability. Priced between $7 and $10 for a large spool.

Cortland Plion I

A premium, low-priced monofilament that's strong enough to land the big ones, yet limp enough to cast with terrific control. Eliminates the curling and coiling characteristics of most monofilament line. Prices run between $7 and $10 for a large spool.

Cortland Plion Monofilament

Berkley TriMax

Bagley's Silver Thread Copolymer Line

Smaller diameters and superior knot strengths in this bonded fishing line. $8 and up for $250-yard spools.

BEST FOR BEGINNERS

Maxima Monofilament

This sturdy lower-priced line is built tough to withstand the abrasion of the bottom- and bait-fishing that younger and beginning fishermen often prefer. The monofilament is chemically treated to cause the line to change color in different types of light, making it difficult for fish to see. Also available in Maxima Ultragreen super-soft monofilament for anglers who concentrate on spinning and plug-casting, and need more pliable line for casting power. From $5 for 250-yard spools up to $15, and $20 in the heavier pound tests on 66-yard spools.

The Business End

Most anglers soon master the basics of rigging "terminal tackle"—the various sinkers, swivels, hooks, lures, and other gadgets attached to the end of the fishing line. But the more an angler knows about how different elements of terminal tackle work, the more access he will have to different fishing opportunities. Plenty of fishermen balk at testing new kinds of water and fish because they don't know how to "rig up," and are reluctant to reveal their ignorance. In this short section, THE FISHING TACKLE CATALOG uses the age-old formula of "form follows function" to explain how the thousands of little metal and plastic things fall into a handful of basic categories.

HOOKS

There are only a handful of established and completely reliable hook manufacturers in the world, and, unfortunately, there are thousands and thousands of variations in hook sizes, patterns, finishes, materials, and quality. The safest way to negotiate the sharp edges of the fishing-hook market is to stick with the proven winners.

Mustad, Eagle Claw, Tru Turn, and some hand-made hook manufacturers, such as Partridge in England, pretty much control the world market of quality hooks, yet each manufacturer has their own system for numbering and categorizing hooks. Hook patterns are the only design-constant among manufacturers. Whenever ordering hooks from a catalog, be sure to specify your desired size and pattern as specifically as possible: There are so many variations! It's always a good idea to include the order number to be doubly sure.

The parts of a hook, as they are discussed by veteran anglers, break down this way: the spearhead, bend, barb, shank, gap, bite, and eye. The point is the sharp tip of the hook; the barb is the sharp edge at reverse angle to the point, the spearhead encompasses the point and barb; the bend is the curved section of the hook; and the shank is the straight section leading to the eye, which attaches to the line, or snell. The gap is the distance between the point and the shank, and the bite is the distance between the point and the lowest point of the bend.[13]

Most hooks are made of carbon, stainless steel, or an alloy of the two. The strength and brittleness of the hook depends on the quality of the steel used in the hook's construction, and on the quality of the manufacturer's hardening and tempering processes. Nickel alloy is still used in some hooks, but while corrosion-proof, it is expensive and relatively heavy. Many anglers believe that carbon-steel hooks are superior to stainless steel hooks in strength, hardness, and sharpness, and while this was true in the past, technological improvements in stainless steel extrusion and hardening by most hook makers have raised stainless steel standards to carbon steel levels in virtually every performance category.[14]

The softness (or brittleness) of a hook's steel is defined by its tempering—the heat treatment of the wire after it has been formed into shape. Over-tempered hooks are brittle, and will easily break on snags or the bony mouth of a fish. Soft hooks will bend, and lose their shape. The leading manufacturers produce hooks of reliable temper, though in some situations anglers may choose soft-temper hooks when fishing among heavy structure or weeds: If snagged, the soft hook can be bent open and pulled away. Similarly, anglers after tarpon or other large fish with extremely bony jaws, will choose highly-tempered, even slightly brittle hooks to gain more penetrating power when they set the hook.

Knowledgeable fishermen will choose hooks "customized" with honed points and barbs for different kinds of hook-setting action.

Spear and Rolled: Difficult to set, but difficult for fish to expel after penetration.

Hollow: Fast, clean penetration, but must be kept razor-sharp to be at all effective.

Barbless: Wreaks less damage to the fish's jaw, allows easier release. Featured in flies for catch-and-release trout fishing.

Knife-edge: The outside edges of the hook point are filed to razor sharpness to faciliate penetration of armored, bony jaws.[15]

Nothing determines the ability of an individual fish hook to do its job more than its pattern and bend. Hook patterns were, for the most part, established by late eighteenth and early nineteenth century tradesmen in England, the industrial European center for hookmaking at that time. Today's Eagle Claw, Mustad, and other manufacturers follow universal pattern specifications in the production and marketing of their various hooks. But, they do not always assign the same number to hooks of the same size. Generally, this rule holds true: The smaller the number, the larger the hook. Most (but not all) manufacturers use the zero system, with the largest hook listed as "1", and numbers going up as 1/0, 2/0, 3/0, etc. to reflect decreasing hook sizes. In general, with the exception of largemouth bass in freshwater and tarpon in saltwater, use the smallest effective hook possible. A small hook means your bait, or lure, will appear more natural, the fish will have an easier time bringing the hook into its mouth, and you will have an easier time removing the hook.

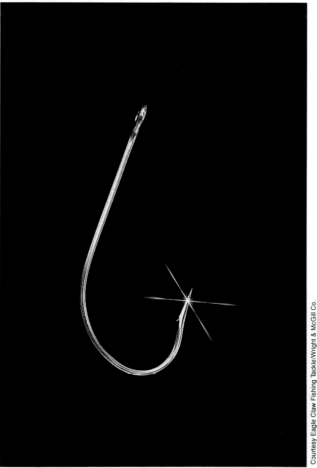

Courtesy Eagle Claw Fishing Tackle/Wright & McGill Co.

Sharply honed, strong hooks can mean the difference between landing or losing a leaping gamefish such as this champion rainbow trout.

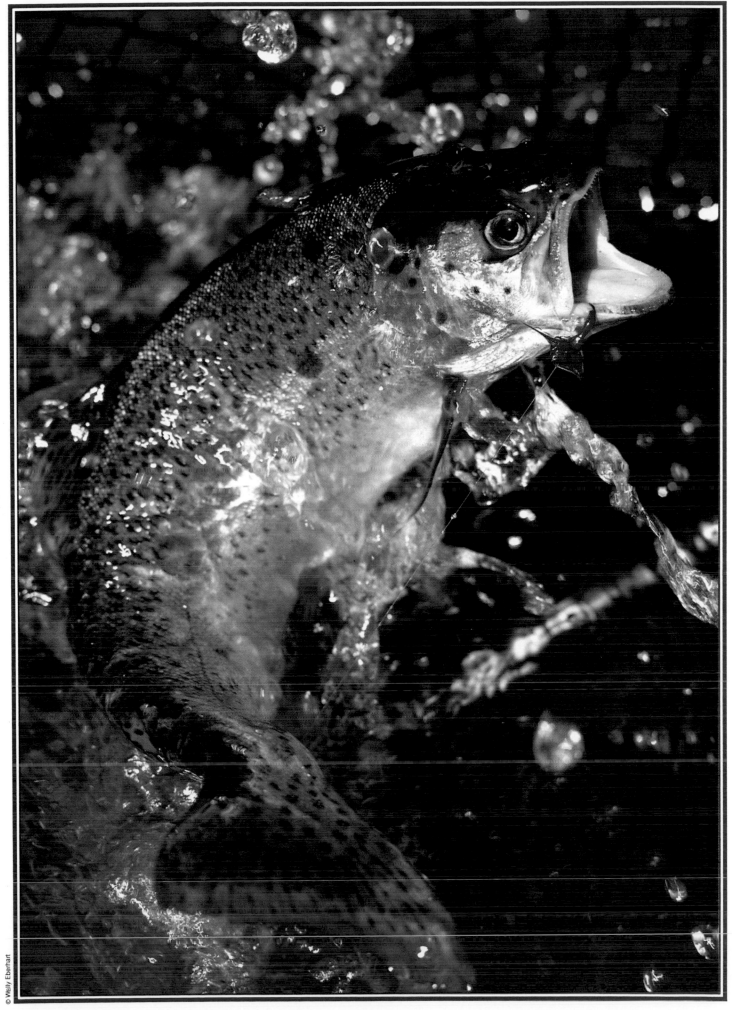

© Wally Eberhart

Here are the popular hook patterns for saltwater and freshwater rigs, with a few eccentric examples thrown in for perspective.

Trust any hooks from these manufacturers: Wright-McGill, Mustad, V.M.C., Partridge, Tru-Turn, and Wilson-Allen.

Mustad Beak/Wright & McGill Eagle Claw

These are nearly identical patterns that are extremely popular among fresh and saltwater fishermen. This is a top still and bait-fishing hook that is also used extensively for trolling. The curved, spearpoint, rolled point will hold reliably in the fish's jaw after the strike, but will not penetrate as easily as other, straighter spearpoints. The hook point is curved to follow the angle or pull an angler places on the line and hook when striking the fish.

Sproat

The Sproat serves exceedingly well in most freshwater angling situations. The wide bend holds the bait away from the shaft for more natural presentation, and provides more leverage for the fish's mouth to take in the spearhead. A highly popular hook for fly-tiers, the wider gap provides room for wide hackle and to tie knots.[16]

Aberdeen

The Aberdeen's slightly squarish bend is similar to the European ''Model Perfect'' pattern. The long shank makes the Aberdeen the perfect hook for baiting up minnows, and the light wire avoids excessive wear on the minnow, allowing it to live longer. The Eagle Claw Aberdeen is tempered to bend before breaking, which makes it a perfect hook for fishing in weeds and other cover. Perfect ice-fishing hook.[17]

O'Shaughnessy

This is the most popular saltwater hook, according to most tackle professionals and fishing writers. The point is bent slightly inward, but, otherwise, the O'Shaughnessy resembles the Sproat and Limerick patterns. Generally an extra-heavy strength hook, preferred for dressing big, wet flies and streamers, bait fishing for larger saltwater bottom feeders, and trot-line fishing. Cadmium-tin plated to protect against corrosion. Made with extra-large eyes for trot lines.

Carlisle

This pattern features an extra-long shank and straight offset point, and is especially effective for fishing with nightcrawlers and minnows. Its length helps prevent the fish from swallowing the hook. Generally for lighter freshwater fishing.

Limerick

Highly popular with fly-tiers and fly-fishermen. Limerick hooks feature a sharp parabolic bend that limits their strength and ability to hold heavy fish. However, the wide gap makes fly-tying easier.

Model Perfect

This is another very popular hook pattern for fly-tiers, with its perfectly symmetrical round bend.

Siwash or Salmon

In widespread use among salmon, steelhead, striped-bass, and bluefish anglers, the Siwash is a strong saltwater hook with a short shank, long point, and a deep bite that active, jumping fish will have difficulty spitting loose.

Salmon Egg

New salmon egg hooks feature a turned-up eye for better striking leverage, and an extra-wide bite for natural presentation of the egg. Generally used for trout and salmon fishing. Some models are built with an additional bait barb on the shank to make the egg more secure. The short shank can mean missed strikes, however.

Pike

The pike hook is designed to fit the long snout of the pike. With the elongated gap, the northern or muskie can inhale the impaled minnow without pushing the hook away in the act. A favorite ice-fishing hook for pike and pickerel.[18]

Chestertown

The long shank and narrow bite on this offset hook—point is curved off-center—is designed to fit a flounder's small mouth.

Tuna Circle

This specialty hook is designed for trot- and long-line commercial fishermen. With the Tuna Circle, tuna, cod, halibut, hakes, and

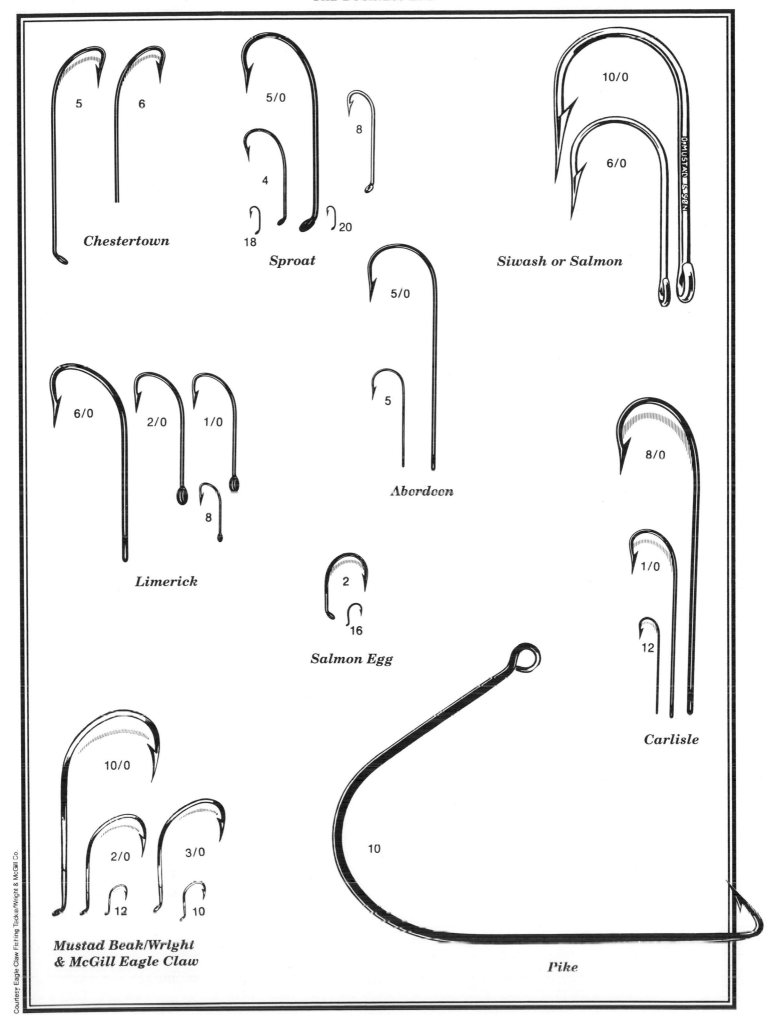

Chestertown

Sproat

Siwash or Salmon

Limerick

Aberdeen

Salmon Egg

Carlisle

Mustad Beak/Wright
& McGill Eagle Claw

Pike

other fish take a long time getting hooked on the trot line, but few of them will escape once they have. Greater holding power, fewer lost fish, and less lost bait: If you're aiming to bring home enough fish to make a living, this hook deserves your attention.

Aberdeen Cricket Hook

This specialty hook is a favorite of bluegill and red-ear anglers who thread up crickets as bait. This hook has a thin, narrow shank with small gap.

Worm Hooks

These are designed to hold large, plastic worms and salamanders. Their curved shanks hold the worm in the right position to create maximum bass-attracting action, and effectively set the hook on strike when the bass inhales the whole worm.

.45 Automatic

This Eagle Claw brand was forged with a special "Z" bend that will prevent the plastic bait from slipping down the shank. Sweeping rotational curve of the hook places the point in position for penetration from any angle.

The Messler

Twisted shank creates easy penetration. The compound curve automatically turns the hook point to enter the bass' jaw when the hook is set. The Messler is designed for "Texas style" worm rigs.

Mustad Central Draught

The slim gap and slight curve of the shank allows proper plastic-worm rigging and makes an easy fit for the bass' mouth.

Trebles

Most treble models are honed with hollow or rolled points, short shanks, and wide rounded bends.

Double baitholders

These double hooks are often honed with hollow or rolled points. They are designed with long shanks for rigging crayfish, grasshoppers, frogs, and other unwieldly live baits. A variety of double hooks, fitted with loops, pins, barbs, and short hooks for securing baits, are on the market from companies like Mister Twister, V.M.C., and Mustad.

Weedless

These long shank, hollow-point, medium-gap hooks are fitted with plastic or metal weed guards from the eye to the point, for easier trolling, casting, and bait fishing in weeds, logs, trees, stumps, rocks, lily pads, and moss. Aberdeen, Sproat, and Limerick patterns are popular weedless styles.

The Mustad, Beak/Wright, and McGill Eagle Claw hooks are often used in spinning and spoon lures. This angler is landing a brown trout.

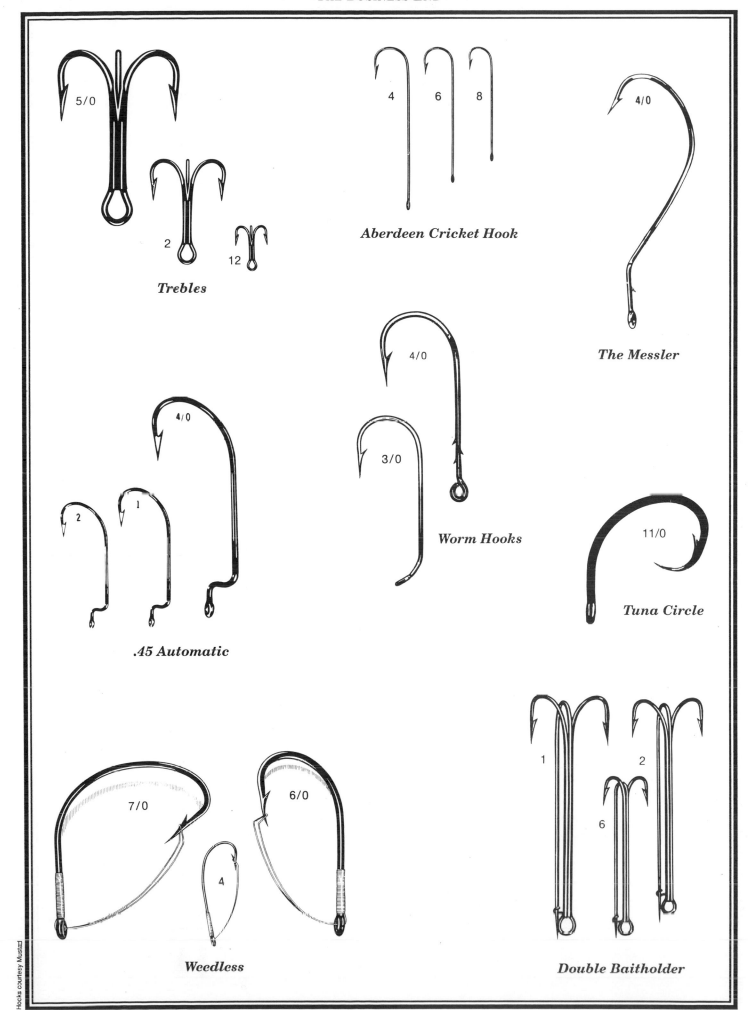

5/0

2

12

Trebles

4   6   8

Aberdeen Cricket Hook

4/0

The Messler

4/0

2   1

.45 Automatic

4/0

3/0

Worm Hooks

11/0

Tuna Circle

7/0

6/0

4

Weedless

1   2

6

Double Baitholder

SINKERS

If you like to bottom-fish, troll, drift-cast, or jig, sinkers are an important part of your life. Trolling sinkers improperly linked to swivels or snaps, or rigged without them, will destroy the fish-attracting action of any bait or lure.

Serious anglers make judicious use of sinkers, and nothing gives away a novice like a bait rig tied to a sinker the size of a Civil War cannonball. There are a number of important principles the situation angler should learn in choosing sinkers.

The first principle in choosing a sinker in fresh or saltwater fishing is to choose a sinker that performs its job with as little weight as possible. The second principle is to match the design of the sinker to the type of bottom terrain in which you'll be trying to catch fish. The third principle is realizing that sinker rigs can be designed to hold baits and lures at specific depths. Trolling requires specialized rig designs in which sinkers are used to hold the lure or bait down where the fish are.

Use as little weight as possible. Fish will not only drop a bait or lure that is unnaturally heavy, but you also don't want to ruin the prospect of fighting a solid gamefish because he or she is dragging an anvil around in the water. The less weight you use, the more likely you are to get hook-ups. Experiment when casting to find the lightest rig that will hold your bait where you want it.

Choose the right design. Smooth, rounded, or cylindrical sinkers such as the dropsey, egg, pencil, cylinder, or tube sinkers aren't as likely to snag where the underwater terrain is broken, rough, rocky, involves coral or other obstructions. Pointed, pyramid and block sinkers are best to use when you need to anchor your rig in sandy or soft ocean, lake, or river bottoms.

Baits and lures can be "sinker-set" at various depths. In drift fishing, for example, the angler chooses a sinker weight that keeps his bait or lure just off the river bottom where it can drift "naturally" with the current, but under the angler's control. In surf-fishing, light sinkers can keep bait suspended in the waves where it will look like real live fish to striped bass or bluefish. Where bait or lues will be most effectively displayed slowly "swimming" in the current, drifting in the tide or otherwise suspended in middle or deep water, sinkers can be used. Pencil and other wrap-around sinkers are the most popular choice for sinker-setting.

SNAPS AND SWIVELS

Both swivels and snaps are particularly important in saltwater and freshwater trolling. Quality swivels are crucial to effective light spinning, and can save surf casters a great deal of aggravation. Snaps save anglers time and effort in any situation where a tackle change must be made quickly.

The more the situational angler knows about snaps and swivels, the more fish-catching rigs and lures will be at his or her disposal. Snaps are a more versatile element of terminal tackle than swivels. In trolling, snaps allow the tackle master to change lures and baits, flashers, dodgers, floats, and weights in a fraction of the time knots would require. Snaps allow easy release of high-cuspid, ornery, and large fish.[19]

But, snaps cannot handle too much punishment, and can break open or apart when a big fish is on. There will be a few times—not many—when a snap costs you a fish. Snaps can hamper lure or bait action if not chosen and rigged properly, and any snap too large for the rig below it will considerably dampen lure movement and piscine interest. Spin-fishermen in particular must choose their snaps (and swivels) with care: a snap placed directly above the lure will effectively turn it off, and snaps too bulky or weighty for a light freshwater outfit will twist line and alter proper movement.

Most snaps are composed of carbon-steel or stainless steel wire, with a brass body. They

Left: *Snap swivels save the angler time when changing or modifying rigs. Many brands, however, are of poor manufacture and not reliable under pressure. Berkley snaps and bead chain swivels are leading brands among experienced surf casters.*

are customarily plated with nickel, chrome, or copper, and are usually finished through an oxide, burnishing, or painting process that produces a variety of colors. Finishing either protects the snap against corrosion for saltwater use, dulls the metal finish to discourage false strikes from game fish, or encourages purchasing strikes from shopping fishermen. While most two piece snaps are made with brass hoods, stainless steel and carbon-steel (spring-tempered to prevent rust and corrosion) wire is stronger and lighter. Brass wire is very weak, and snaps showing brass wire should be avoided.[20]

Snaps are available from different manufacturers in a variety of non-uniform sizes unique to each maker. To find the right size snap for your lures and rigs, check with your local tackle shop owner. Snaps are identified by test strength, which allows you to approximately match it to your rig. Be as precise as possible in using the smallest and safest snap for the fish you expect to catch.

Like "snap," the word "swivel" is onomatopoeic: its name is its function. Swivels are

Left: *Offshore swivels are usually made of brass, with extremely high breaking strength.* Below: *A charter mate cleaning a salmon on one of Oregon's hundreds of offshore salmon trollers.* Bottom: *Any veteran surf caster will know the fish finder rig, which frees the action of hook and line from the sinker.* Right: *Ocean-going wreck, reef and bottom bouncing, and drift-fishing charters will often rig up with three-way swivels and rigs to give customers the chance to get multiple hook-ups of flounder, porgies, and other bottom feeders.*

© Allan Wetz

strategically placed in rigs to facilitate the revolving motion of key elements in the terminal tackle, and to prevent line twist in trolling rigs and spinning line and lures. The leading manufacturers are the ever-present Sampo, Berkley, Pompanette, and Bead Chain, the same folks who bring you the bead-chain light cord in your bathroom.

Swivels are not created alike. Many poorly-made swivels won't swivel unless the entire rig is moving at a fair rate of speed. This can be devastating news if you happen to be trolling for tarpon or other fish that like slow-moving baits. The better the bearings within the swivel, the easier it will be for the swivel to do its job. Smaller swivels swivel better than large swivels, but the more weight dragged in the rig, the larger the swivel needs to be. Smaller swivels will lock up under heavy rig loads. Use the smallest rotating swivel possible in putting together your spinning rigs.

Single and split-head **barrel** swivels differ in the number of eye shanks forged to the slider bearings within the swivel hood, and the double shanks of the **split-head** swivel increase its strength. **Bead-chain** swivels are much more flexible and translate action to the terminal bait or lure very effectively—and the small, smooth bead hoods virtually never snag. Bead-chain swivels are the best choice in all but the lightest spinning rigs. When you decide to buy high-quality bead-

chain swivels, that means the Bead Chain tackle company. Cheaper brands can snap off under pressure because the metal used in the hoods pops open under line pull, or the linking wire fails. **Box** swivels are an open-bodied form of the barrel swivel.

Offshore swivels are the big daddies of the swivel set. Made of brass, offshore swivels are very flat, smooth, and closely mated, with extremely high breaking strength. The importance of tackle strength in big-game fishing has kept the shoddy makers out of offshore swivels, and these will be reliable virtually anywhere they can be found.[21]

Ball-bearing swivels are the most reliable and, when made well, most expensive fresh and light-saltwater swivels. Sampo ball bearings are the most efficient swivels by far, and the most expensive.[22] Sampos turn easily, providing swivel at amazingly slow speeds above light line, lures, and leaders. Sampos are well-suited to light-tackle spinning rigs where repeated spinner or plug casting will twist mono until line curling and looping make long casts and tight-line retrieves difficult.

Three way swivels are produced for sinker and trolling rigs, allowing anglers to make multiple tackle hook-ups at a single point in the rig.

Recommended manufacturers: Sampo, Bead Chain, Berkley, and Pompanette, a saltwater specialty snap.

GOURMET RIGS FOR BOTTOM FEEDERS

One of the situational angler's greatest arts is the construction of sinker and bait rigs. While every sea salt has his favorite tackle set-ups for bottom trolling, flounder, or float rigging, hundreds of years of angling tradition have established reliable rigging methods for presenting live bait to bottom-feeding or bottom-prowling piscine prey. The more you baitfish, the more creative you will become in designing your own rigs, but here are some universally-acclaimed terminal-tackle set ups to immediately add to your repertoire.

The Basic Bottom Fisher

Attach a three way swivel to the line, add a bank sinker and snelled hook to each eye. Use from boats for bottom bouncing and drifting, or still fishing from docks and piers.

Break-Away Rig

When fishing rough bottoms, wrecks, reefs, or other heavily obstructed environments, anglers tie the sinker to break off when it gets snagged—so the entire rig is not lost. Connect the fishing line to a hook with a swivel and then tie the sinker to the swivel with a light piece of monofilament.

Sliding Sinker Rig

A flexible bottom rig for all kinds of deep-water baitfishing. The line is linked to the swivel with a snelled hook below. An egg sinker is strung above the swivel, which slides up and down the fishing line, so the fish won't feel the weight when it takes the bait.

© David E. Rowley/Envision

Spreader Rig

Now you can fish two, three, or even four baits at once from the same rod and reel without tangling or line crossing. Is it great sport? No. Does it catch many fish? Yes. The fishing line is tied to a spreader, which is a swivel with jutting wire arms that end in round eyes. Join snelled hooks to the round eyes. A crosslock or Pompanette snap joins a dropsey sinker to the bottom of the spreader swivel. Bon appetit!

Bottom-Trolling Rig

For those gamers that work the lower depths. From the bottom up, rig it this way: A jig, feather, or spoon will be trolled behind a 3- to 25-foot leader of mono or wire, depending on the dental work of the prey. The leader links to a bead-chain swivel to facilitate line rotation, which links to a torpedo or keel sinker attached to another bead-chain swivel joined to the main line. Depending on the trolling depth required, lead core or wire lines may be necessary.

Deep-Trolling Rig

In this rig, the bait or lure is trolled as deep as need be, but the leader and fishing line are joined by a three-way swivel from which a dropsey sinker is trailed to keep the lure or bait off the bottom.

Fluke Rig

The fishing line is joined to a leader with a three way swivel, from which a dropsey or bank sinker is tied to sink the rig. A spinning flasher is mounted above the hook to attract the attention of lethargic, weird-looking flounder. Use as many spinners or flashers as you like.

Fish-Finder Rig

Favored by surf casters, this set-up frees the action of the hook and line from the sinker, which is attached to the line above the swivel via a connecting link snap. Pyramid sinkers are preferred for their anchoring ability in soft sand. The bait floats free in the water, often bouyed off the bottom with a float or cork attached to the swivel. Fish will dine on your bait with no "sinker sense"— which means that you will eventually dine on them.[23]

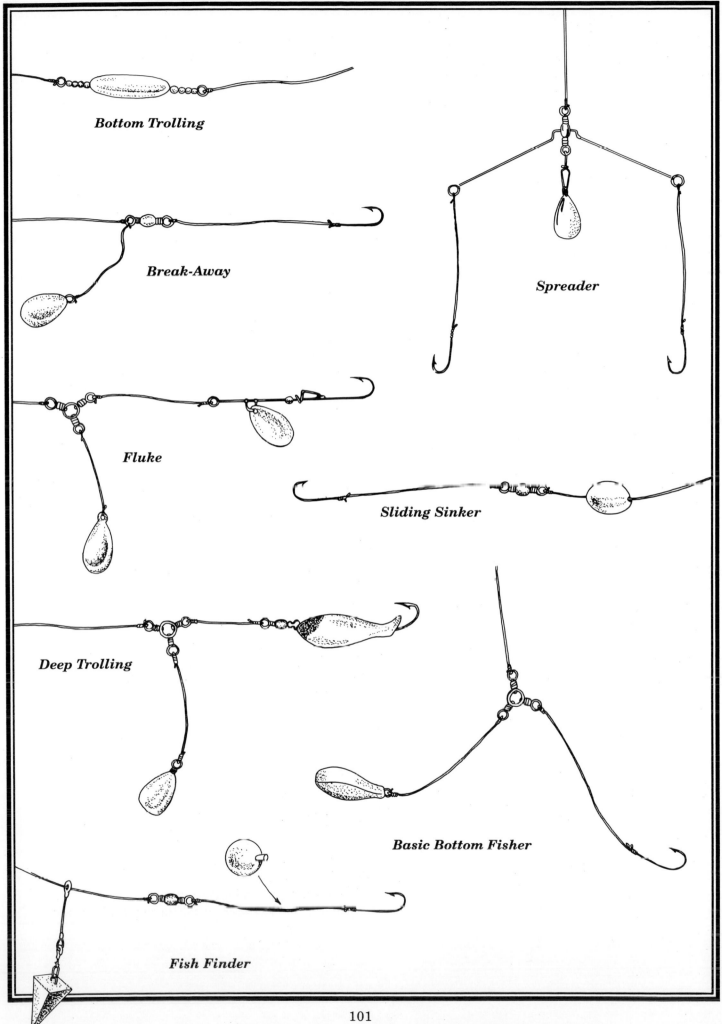

Bottom Trolling

Break-Away

Spreader

Fluke

Sliding Sinker

Deep Trolling

Basic Bottom Fisher

Fish Finder

CHAPTER SIX

Drawing the Strike

"I am convinced that fish strike at baits and lures for many reasons other than to feed upon them. I think it is likely that most of the time factors other than predatory ones are involved in strikes against artificial lures. Curiousity, fear, anger, self defense, territorial defense, petulance—all these things can cause a fish to attack a lure."
—Gary Soucie, author of *Hook, Line, & Sinker*

What makes one lure more appealing than another? Why are certain types of lures more effective? When do fish prefer live bait over lures? What are the different types? Why are lures effective at one time and not another?

The number of lures available to the fisherman pursuing America's better game fish number in the thousands, as do the questions anglers ask about them—whether dry flies or buzz baits, popping plugs, or floating divers. Even the lightly-seasoned angler knows that virtually any lure can bag a desired fish, if presented at the right time of day during the right time of the year, and fished in the proper manner. In other words,

even shoddy lures will work if matched to the fishing situations where they can perform to best advantage. But it is something like a law of physics that certain lures possess sheer fish-attracting magic. Every fisherman has a plug or spinner in his tackle box that always seems to catch fish when everything else fails. When thousands of fishermen find themselves using the same "secret weapon," the conclusion can be drawn that this lure is special. Anglers all have their private lures that seem to work for them and no one else, and certainly this quality of idiosyncrasy adds to the interest.

Good lures catch nothing but floating branches and beer cans if they are not effectively used. But as a musician must know scales, an angler must understand how fish behave, what influences their feeding habits, and how they relate to their environment.

Here, I unveil some of the "secret weapons" that have delivered results again and again in America's multitudinous proving waters. Most of the lures presented have caught fish for thousands of fishermen for many years. They are top-sellers; they are used by guides and professionals, and they are classics.

A SHOWCASE OF CLASSIC LURES

SWIMMING PLUGS

The word plug describes any lure shaped to imitate a small fish, or other swimming, amphibious life (such as frogs, reptiles, eels), that when retrieved "swims" on top or beneath the water in an action suggesting the actual movements of the imitated fish. Swimming plugs run beneath the surface, either shallow or deep.[24] The selection here has been restricted to those plugs that swim relatively close to the surface. Deep-swimming, sinking plugs (or "crank baits") are mentioned below.

Rapala
Freshwater and Saltwater

These beautifully shaped, paint-finished wood, swimming minnows are produced by the same people who designed the first fishing plug. Original inventor Karl Rapala has died, but his family continues to build, design, paint, and test these lures of world-wide reknown in their Finland factory. Rapala means quality craftsmanship. Rapala means trued and balanced swimming lures that impart just the right underwater action. Available in dozens of sizes, colors, patterns, and swimming depths. Excellent in various styles for all kinds of game fish, Rapala

produces lures in sinking, floating, floatings diving, and popping styles. Perhaps no lure presents such highly realistic "swimming" action as the Rapala. Styles include: Floating Minnow, Countdown Sinking Minnow, Muskie 13 Floating Minnow, Magnum, and Sliver.

Creek Chub Pikie
Freshwater and Light Saltwater

This venerable, wood-carved, classic lure has been a favorite of anglers throughout the North Woods and Northwest for over fifty years. Reliable standbys for pike and muskie, the Pikie is effective for catching most large game fish—from bass to salmon. Sizes run from 3¼ to 6 inches for one of the largest freshwater plugs available. The Creek Club Pikie swims a few inches below the surface.

Lazy Ike
Freshwater

These deadly minnow imitators have been a standard of tackle boxes for over thirty-five years. The flat, curved plug produces a frantic swimming action that looks like a struggling minnow. It runs just beneath the surface. This is a good plug for bass and large

Rapala

trout, and is extremely effective in larger sizes for pike and muskie. Available in sizes from 1¹⁄₆ to 3⅓ inches.

Luhr Jensen J-Plug
Freshwater and Saltwater

This diving and darting plug is highly popular for trolling and casting and is used all over the country by salmon, lake trout, and steelhead fishermen. The J-Plug is noted for its irresistable power to attract active game fish. When the finny marauders are hitting, they go crazy over the J-Plug.

Les Davis Witch Doctor
Freshwater and Saltwater

This is one of the most popular swimming plugs in the Northwest and Canada for salmon. The Witch Doctor, in its four sizes that range from ¼ to 2¾ ounces, also draws lake trout, striped bass, snook, steelhead, and larger bass. It is popular with Canadian anglers seeking

Cisco Kid Salty Husky

the Kamloops trout. This plug can reach a depth of 15 feet when trolled.

FLOATING DIVERS

Floating divers rest on the surface after the cast, and then, during the retrieve, dive underwater and run a few feet beneath the surface. The rule of thumb is to fish floating divers with a medium-slow, herky-jerky retrieve—but, as always, observe the results of each fishing situation and adjust. Rapid jerks of the rod will impart frantic, fish-attracting action to these plugs.

Heddon Wood Vamp
Freshwater and Saltwater

One of the greatest big-fish catchers of all time, the Heddon Wood Vamp was introduced in the 1920s and is still a mainstay of tackle boxes today. The Vamp rests on the surface and works down to a depth of 3 feet when retrieved. It is a joined, two-piece plug with treble hooks. Effective on pike, big bass, muskies, walleye, striped bass, and even snook.

SINKING PLUGS
(Crank baits)

Sinking plugs, or crank baits as they are often called, are designed to run deep—up to 20 feet when retrieved on a shore cast, and up to depths of 30 or 40 feet when trolled. Different plugs reach varying depths, depending on design. These plugs are popular for reaching freshwater pelagic fish such as lake trout and salmon. Most plug manufacturers design crank baits to run at different depths, so buy the plug that will sink to the levels of the fish you are trying to catch. In lakes, large rivers, and reservoirs, fish will seek the thermocline, the most oxygenated layer of water.

Luhr-Jensen J-Plug

Cotton Cordell Wally Diver
Freshwater

Equipped with a built-in, fish-attracting rattle and deep-diving plastic lip, the Wally Diver is a great, sinking crank bait. The Wally Diver can reach salmon, lake trout, and walleye even in the heat of summer, running up to 12-feet deep on an average cast, and over 30 feet on a flat-line troll. Weighs ⅜ of an ounce and is 4½ inches long.

Natural Ike
Freshwater

The Natural Ike started one of the few real departures in lure design. Lazy Ike came up with the idea of creating deep-running, high-action lures with a photo-generated finish that created a lifelike look, complete with scales, and gill covers. Imitators rushed in, but the Natural Ike still leads sales in lifelike imitation lures. Sizes range from 1⅝ to 3 inches in a small range of baitfish 'styles.'

Cisco Kid Salty Super Husky
Saltwater

Technically a sinking plug, the Cisco Kid is often a first choice among fishing captains for medium-depth plug trolling. Effective on tarpon, grouper, and king mackerel.

POPPERS

The popper is a surface-disturbing plug. It creates interest with our scaly friends by gurgling, bubbling, and "popping" on the water surface when the angler retrieves the plug. When fishing any popping plug, it is of the essence to allow the plug to sit on the surface after the cast. Most strikes arrive before retrieve. Give the fish time to see it! If a minute or two passes without a hit, begin your retrieve, jerking the plug so the open face gurgles and pops in the surface water. After a few "pops", rest the lure. Fish will often strike after the first or second series of retrieves.

Arbogast Hula-Popper

Cotton Cordell Pencil Popper
Saltwater

Excellent for bringing striped bass to the surface, this is a popular surf-casting plug.

Hula-Popper
Freshwater

The Hula-Popper is a piece of vintage Americana. Its familiar red-and-white body and "hula" skirt have been a friendly sight to fishermen since the plug was introduced in 1938. Of course, it is available in a number of patterns. Sizes run from small lures of 1¼ inches and ³/₁₆ of an ounce up to 2¼ inches at ⅝ of an ounce. This is America's most popular freshwater popper.

Gaines Spin Popper
Freshwater

These bass lures are a cross between a bass bug and popper plug. Larger than any bass bug, these lure work on the surface, their cupped faces create disturbances that bass will notice. Designed for use with medium-action spinning gear. Available in cupped head, sliding head, and skipping head designs.

Stan Gibbs Polaris
Saltwater

This lure is very effective on blues and striped bass. Designed for long-distance casting, surf casters use a herky-jerky, medium-speed retrieve to give the lure maximum action on the surface.

Super Striper Popper
Saltwater

Brings them to the surface fast and frenzied. When the stripers are active, this lure can't miss. The Super Striper Popper is among the most popular of the surf-casting poppers used on the East Coast.

CHUGGERS

Chuggers are high-tech poppers. The chugger is retrieved on the surface like a popper, but it is fitted with blades, a propeller, or an extra fin on the nose of the plug that stirs com-

motion in the water as you slowly and steadily crank it home. Great for night fishing.

Arbogast Jitterbug
Freshwater

This is one of the easiest to use and most effective plugs ever designed. First sold in 1938, the Jitterbug produces plenty of surface commotion as it is reeled back across the surface of the water. The blades screwed to its snout gurgle and pop in the water to suggest a wounded bait fish or an amphibian high-tailing it for cover. This is the lure that will probably catch more bass at night than any other—and the simple cast and retrieve mechanics required to work the plug make it easy to use when you can't see past the tip of your nose. The Jitterbug runs the gamut of sizes, from 1¼ to 4 inches.

Gag's Grabber

Cotton Cordell Pencil Popper

SPOONS

The spoon is the simplest and perhaps the most effective of the fishing lures. The bent blade of the spinning spoon simply wobbles back and forth under retrieve to make what is by all accounts a highly lifelike imitation of a minnow.

Heddon Crazy Crawler

Heddon Crazy Crawler
Freshwater

Another very popular surface disturber, the Crazy Crawler is fitted with a pair of hinged metal vanes to stir up a commotion on the surface. What does it imitate? A strange black frog? A stubby minnow? A fearsome round insect? No one can say for certain, but it does catch fish, especially at night. Should be retrieved steadily so the wings churn the water.

JERK BAITS

Jerk baits are large top-water plugs used almost exclusively for pike and muskies.

Old Wooden Bait Company Muskie Lures

These handmade lures feature glass eyes, brass lips, brass

hook hangers, and wire construction. Ranging from 5½ to 8 inches long, these beautiful plugs are effective muskie-catching tools.

STICK BAITS

These are surface-disturbing plugs that offer no action except that which the angler imparts to them with the rod tip. Very effective when imparted with lively rips and jerks of the rod. Don't jerk the plug wildly, but give it the lifelike erratic and irregular twitches of a needlefish in trouble.

Gag's Grabbers Needlefish
Saltwater

Wooden-needlefish stick plug features wire construction, extra-heavy-duty hardware, and hooks.

Eppinger Daredevle
Freshwater and Saltwater

This is the best-known lure in America. The red-and-white striped spoon with the familiar, jaunty devil's head imprinted on the blade has caught more fish—and spent more time in more tackle boxes—than any other American lure ever made. And for good reason. This simple lure design, in all its various color patterns, has received high praise from fishermen from all over the country, for many, many years. Whenever you find yourself getting "blanked" on the water, switch to the Eppinger lure and see if your luck doesn't change. The wiggling spoon imparts the erratic, frantic, nervous action of a wounded or struggling bait fish that is easy prey for all the great game fish of any size—trout, bass, walleye, pike, musky, or salmon.

Arbogast Jitterbug

Cather's Spoons
Freshwater and Saltwater

These spoons have demonstrated impressive results in bagging freshwater and saltwater game fish, especially blues, trout, and bass.

Bridgeport Diamond Jig

JIGS

A jig is a weighted lure consisting of a metal (usually lead) head to which a bucktail, feather, or nylon skirt is attached. Most anglers agree that the fish-catching qualities of jigs, which are considerable, lie in its ability to approximate the sudden movements of bait fish through bright, flashing colors and stop-and-go action. The jig elicits sudden, aggressive strikes, often "annoying" sensitive predators into action.

Dan Gapen Sr.'s Ugly Bug
Freshwater

This imitation jig, which imitates a combination of a hellgrammite, a crawfish, and a water dog, has won legions of supporters who pull legions of smallmouth and walleye from lakes and rivers with this versatile lure.

Stanley Metal Flake Flippin' Jig
Freshwater

A rubber skirt is splashed with metal flake to catch light and attract strikes. The nylon-bristle weed guard protects against snags without interfering with hook-ups. A proven bass catcher.

Hopkins No-Eql
Saltwater

Favorite surf cast-casting jigs, the No-Eql can travel far distances on a cast, and its subsurface action is among the most attractive to silvery bait-fish predators such as the bluefish. The No-Eql is retrieved swiftly like a plug; although the angler should impart an up-and-down action for best results.

Bridgeport Diamond Jig
Saltwater

Not really a jig, but one of the all-time-favorite saltwater lures and it's still handmade in America. Its eight sides of highly polished nickel provide maximum light reflection to attract fish. Effective in trolling, casting, or jigging, the Bridgeport jig has been catching fish for over fifty years.

Zing ama Jig
Saltwater

This popular steel surf-casting plug and jig catches weakfish, mackerel, blues, and striped bass. In weights from ⅜ to 3 ounces, the Zing ama Jig is fished at middle and lower depths.

Uncle Buck's Crappie Bug

This jig, tied with a chenille body and a rubber skirt, is available in many colors. The Crappie Bug is death on the water, a panfish terminator.

SPINNERS

A lure consisting of a spinning blade and a tuft of hair, or nylon, complemented with beads and other ornaments. Spinners are among the most popular freshwater lures for panfish and smaller game fish (they're very good on trout). Still, many anglers even prefer spoons in situations where the spinner would be appropriate.

Mepps Aglia Original French Spinner

Treble hooks in various colors: the bestselling artificial lure in the world. A classic of lure design that has been copied by many manufacturers.

Hopkins No-Eql, with Worm

Eppinger Daredevle

Mepps Aglia Spinner

© Tony Cenicola/Lure by Mepps

Les Davis Bolo Spinner

This is one of the few spinners actively and consistently used by experienced big-game fishermen. Very popular in the Northwest, the Bolo attracts all major game fish. The patented slit at the bottom of the blade produces a buzzing effect that attracts fish with sometimes unbelievable intensity—they will hit this spinner hard. Red-tail tags and feathered trebles add strike appeal. Available in sizes that range from $1/16$ to $1/2$ ounce.

Lazy Ike Musky Assassin
Freshwater

This monster spinner is fitted with a huge hank of bucktail to bring the aggressive, meat-eating muskies out from their lairs and cover.

Panther Martin Spinner

The Panther Martin features a rotor-blade spinner that swings around the lure's central wire, rather than an additional clevis. This revolving blade produces the famous Panther Martin "sonic vibrations" that have induced many a young angler to buy the spinner. The Panther Martin has proven very effective, and many young anglers continue to buy the spinner through their fishing adulthood, because it entices strikes from the more active, marauding game fish such as bass, brook trout, and lake trout.

SPINNER BAITS

The spinner bait is a combined lure that matches one or more spinner blades with a jig, connected by a triangular wire that holds them apart.

Mister Twister Spinner Bait
Freshwater

Mister Twister has become the brand name in the manufacture of soft, plastic lures and worms. Spinner baits are also very popular "hawg-bustin" fare, and Mister Twister makes them better than anybody. Spinner baits can be fished at any depth: buzzed at the surface, jigged from the bottom, or spun at middle depths.

Mr. Twister Phenom Worm

Mister Twister Spinner Bait, one of many variations.

Courtesy Luhr-Jensen

Les Davis Bolo Spinner

Double O OH YA Spinner Bait 365-D
Freshwater

This durable spinner bait is the only model ever designed to hold, save, and keep live bait in position. Each bait features a stainless steel ball-bearing swivel, and hand-tied hackle.

PLASTIC WORMS

Plastic and rubber worms have become very popular with largemouth bass fishermen all over America. Made in a dizzying array of colors, shapes, scents, and sizes, manufacturers have developed liquid plastics that give these worms incredibly lifelike feel and swimming appearance in the water. Similarly-designed plastic salamander, crawfish, water puppy, and grub lures are also popular and effective.

Mister Twister
Freshwater

The original. Highly acclaimed by bass, trout, striper, and blues anglers, the Mister Twister has caught dozens of different game fish species. Jigged or tipped to a spinner, this is one of the great high-percentage, take-no-prisoners lures around. Requires careful, slow retrieve.

Mister Twister Phenom Worm
Freshwater

Available in six lengths and fifty-five colors, the Phenom is among Mister Twister's oldest and most popular soft-plastic worms.

Mr. Twister Jig

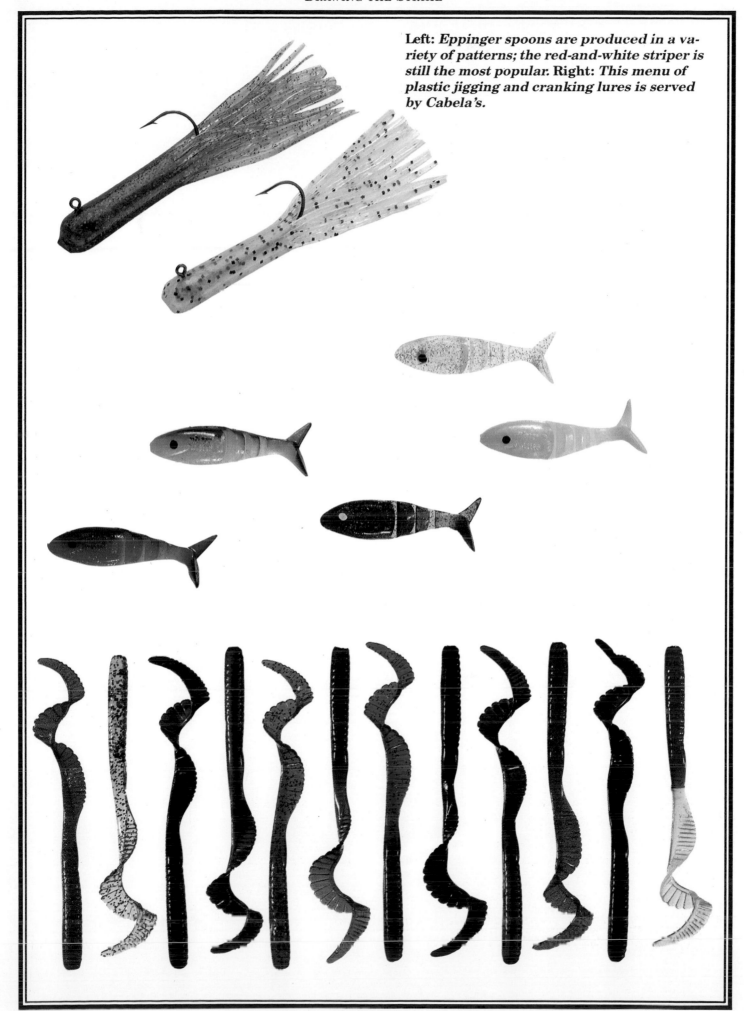

Left: Eppinger spoons are produced in a variety of patterns; the red-and-white striper is still the most popular. Right: This menu of plastic jigging and cranking lures is served by Cabela's.

Fly-Fishing Tackle

"Fly-fishing has over several centuries gathered around itself a mystique, an aroma of almost magical sophistication, that causes it to attract or repel prospective participants more intensely than other types of fishing."—Paul Schullery, *American Fly-fishing: A History.*

Whether you are an experienced or beginning angler, have never heard of fly-fishing, or only tried it once or twice, undertaking the practice of catching trout with a fly could be one of the most rewarding in your sporting life. Don't be intimidated by the voluminous literature surrounding fly-fishing, the precise casting techniques, or boggling array of flies. Fly-fishing is based on a few simple concepts, which, once mastered, provide the thinking angler with all the knowledge needed to pursue the sport and to excel at it.

Fly-fishing does require learning a more complex casting technique than is required for most other styles of fishing. Trout fishermen must commit themselves to a sophisticated understanding of the behavior of their quarry. Anyone watching an experienced fly angler roll and unroll beautiful, precise, arcing casts may feel that learning to fly-cast may be no easier than mastering violin-

making. However, after the caster learns the basic points of technique, and trains his arm and shoulder to follow that motion, (which may initially feel unnatural) he will soon be able to make precise casts. As with any technique in any sport, those who work harder will refine their abilities and reap more rewards. As fly-fishermen improve their technique and learn to catch more fish, they will also want to upgrade their tackle.

Learning, however, isn't fun without rewards. Fly-fishing's rewards come as the angler masters the techniques. Satisfaction comes as the angler conquers casting, learns about the hatches on his local river, trout feeding, and territorial behavior and then uses this knowledge to catch fish. Eventually, many fly-fishermen begin tying their own flies, and enjoy the special thrill of catching large fish on lures of their own creation. (For budding fly tiers there is a short selection of fly-tying materials and kits on page 151.)

If you're considering taking up fly-fishing, begin your career by studying how to use and choose quality fly tackle and read up on the techniques of casting, presentation, imitation, retrieve, and other challenges of fishing for trout in the field. Most of the good how-to fly-fishing books also include basic lessons on trout feeding behavior, trout habitats, hatches, and other subjects surrounding the life, loves, feeding habits, and frustrations of Mr. Salmo.

People become intimately attached to fly tackle in ways that defy description or comparison with other forms of fishing. Fly rods and reels are saved for years as family heirlooms, passed down in wills, and given as presents meant to last a lifetime. Rare fly tackle brings high prices at auctions where collectors bid for antique tackle by makers such as Hardy, Sharpe, and Silex. Fishermen spend winter weekends maintaining and tooling rods and reels that are often used in the field for twenty, thirty, or fifty years. As with wines and musical instruments, certain rod or reel models made in certain years are prized more than others. Rod and reel craftsmen pride themselves on painstaking handmade construction that drives the price of their goods very high.

RODS

Perhaps the most important piece of fly tackle is the rod. Why? Without a rod of proper response, comfort, and flexibility, the fly-fisherman cannot cast well, and, if he cannot cast well, he will probably not catch fish. In theory, the interplay between the motion of the fly rod, and the weight of the fly line as the angler casts, will pay out the line, and deliver it to the intended target.

The word "load" is often used in describing the act of fly-casting. The load of a fly rod refers to how much the weight of the fly line bends the rod as it is backcast—the part of the cast where the angler cocks his arm and fly line behind him to prepare for the forward delivery. The power of the cast results from the springing of the fly rod. The fly-fisherman needs a rod that loads properly for his fly-fishing situations. If the rod cannot deliver the load properly—that is, if the rod does not spring back on the forward part of

© Barry & Cathy Beck Photo

© Barry & Cathy Beck Photo

Good Books on the Basics of Fly-Fishing

....

Trout on a Fly by Lee Wulff
Nick Lyons Books

First Cast: Fly-Fishing for Beginners by Leonard Wright, Jr.
Fireside Books/Simon & Schuster

The L.L. Bean Guide to Fly-Fishing by Dave Whitlock
Nick Lyons Books

Orvis Fly-Fishing Guide by Tom Rosenbauer
Nick Lyons Books

the cast with sufficient power—the leader and the line will not straighten out and reach the intended target. If the rod overpowers the load and snaps too far past the center, the angler will lose casting control and crack flies off tippets, or send leaders into trees.[25]

Fly-fishers stalking the small, silent-running streams of East Coast fisheries such as the Catskills need slow-action fly rods that offer higher response and more flexibility than heavier models. A stiff, reinforced rod butt gives the angler muscle to land bruisers such as this hook-jawed brown trout.

and stick with them for an entire season; so, you must go to the trout; he won't go to you or your fly.

Accurately delivering the fly requires that the fly-fisherman feel extremely comfortable with his rod, that his casting motion is completely automatic, and his mind is free to focus on how to catch trout.

Of course, price *does* play a large role in the kind of fly rod you can get. Do not overspend on tackle until you decide what level of commitment you are willing to make to the sport. But whenever and wherever you buy a fly rod, and whatever you spend on one, don't make the attempt without knowing what makes one rod different from another—and don't buy a rod unless it feels comfortable.

Test drive the fly rods you might buy. Feel the rod's action; gauge its feel for your hand, arm, and casting style. Does it feel too whippy? Too stiff? Does it move too fast or too slow for your casting speed? Do you feel a sense of control? Does it respond to shifts in strength and direction?

There are other, more concrete matters to consider in choosing a fly rod and outfit. You must match your outfit to the situations in which you expect to be fishing. Before buying any equipment, know where you'll be fishing, how big you can expect the average fish to be, and the general pattern of their feeding habits (do they feed on the surface or on the bottom?). Will you need to make short, accurate casts or long-distance ones? Will you need to fish wet flies or dry flies?

Fly-rod design perfectly illustrates the situational principle of fishing. Each rod is shaped by design specifications derived from the fishing environment in which the rod is meant to perform. The elements of rod con-

Many fly-fishing veterans will discuss the "action" of a rod as being fast, medium, or slow. The action of a rod describes how long the rod takes to deliver the load. Slow rods have softer construction, and seem to walk through the casting motion. The loading and delivering of line from back cast to forward cast takes longer to complete. The cast rolls more than it snaps. In general, slower rods are more accurate—or encourage more accurate casts—while faster rods, which hurl the load forward much more quickly, provide the angler with more casting power and distance.

The beginning fly-fisherman should generally look for a balanced, medium-action rod—one that bends back and snaps ahead with a smooth, uniform motion. The casting motion should feel like a pendulum's swing, with the rod arc gently returning to center.

If you plan to take fly-fishing seriously, don't buy an adequate fly rod. Buy a fly rod that suits you perfectly within your chosen price range. Because you simply can't catch trout if you can't place a fly where you want it on stream or lake. Trout are stationary fish. They find holding positions in the water

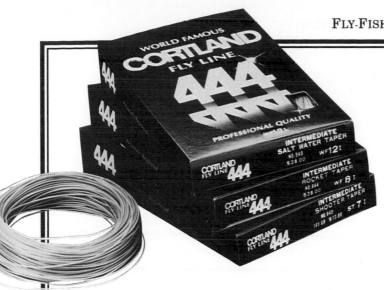

Cortland 444 SL Fly Line

struction that make up each rod's individual "profile" are these: length, strength, stiffness, and the line weight a rod can throw. All of these are affected by the material from which the rod is made—graphite, bamboo, or fiberglass. Lightweight graphite, light-line rods, for instance, are meant to cast accurately over short distances for small trout.

LINE WEIGHT

Rods are designed to throw a specific weight line, and the combination of line weight and rod length determines the rod's action. So let's look at some line weights and what kind of fish they're designed to catch, because if you don't know what line weight you'll be using, you won't know what rod to buy.

Line weights 2 to 4

This lightest fly line is appropriate for sensitive trout waters where the water is narrow and clear, and skittish browns or brookies hole up in shallow stream pockets and pools. There's no talking, splashing, or long casts allowed; the angler must conceal his presence, and this light fly line creates minimum disturbance to the surface of the stream.

These lightweight lines also provide challenge for those fly anglers who want to give the smaller trout a sporting chance. However, in fly-fishing it is always the weight of the line that casts the lure, and this light line is difficult to cast, which makes it less than ideal for the beginning fisherman.

Line weights 4 to 6

This is the best all-around line weight for most trout fishing situations. Best for cast-

ing nymphs and small flies, the 6-weight lines can also horse out the large, bushy flies that catch wind on the cast. The 6-weight line is perfect for the beginner going after anything from brook trout in Upper Michigan, to browns in the Letort River, to the bigger rainbows and cutthroats in Wyoming and Colorado.

Line weights 6 to 8

These lines are designed for the fly-fisherman involved in bigger situations: bigger trout, bigger water, and bigger flies. Depending on the turbulence and breadth of the river being fished, heavier line weights can be more effective on large, Western trout such as lake cutthroats, Lehontan cutthroats, Kamloops trout, and big lake browns. In fast, broad rivers, where the fly-fisherman's mobility is limited, and long casts are required, the fly-fisherman may need to move up to a 7- or 8-weight line to reach distant holding positions.

Where bushy, heavy flies are needed—bass bugs, weighted nymphs, huge mouse and frog flies—the 8-weight lines can handily do the job. In fact, 8-weight line will cast just about any fly that weighs less than a chair!

Line weights 8 to 10

We're talking rope here. The 8- and 9-weights need long, stiff, saltwater rods for effective loading and casting, and are only suitable for the biggest, meanest freshwater trout, steelhead, and salmon. Casting 10-weight line on a light, whippy pole is like using a Yugo to pull a two-ton boat trailer.

© Frank S. Balthis

ROD LENGTH

The function of a rod's length is entwined with its line weight. Generally, heavy line weights need long rods that can generate the momentum needed for casting. Smaller weights don't need as much leverage, but thinner, longer rods can increase the angler's accuracy. Except for those fishermen angling for steelhead and salmon, most fly-fishermen find that the right rod for them is between 7 and 9 feet long. The most popular rod length is 8 to 8½ feet. Some fishermen find that rods much shorter than this (depending on the material used to build them) offer insufficient casting power. The larger rods of 9 to 10 feet, while able to cast small or large flies extraordinarily long distances, pack a lot of firepower, and are notoriously difficult for the beginner to control.

Most beginners choose rods around 8½ feet long that throw 5- or 6-weight line. It's probably best to start looking at rods of this size, and expand your investigation outward.

ROD COMPOSITION

Bamboo

While fiberglass and graphite rods now offer lighter, whippier, and more responsive rods for the money (graphite surpasses bamboo in most measures of rod quality), quality bamboo rods offer the fly-fisherman a chance to buy one of the most carefully constructed, naturally handsome, and wonderfully responsive artifacts in sport.

A bamboo rod is a graceful, beautiful object, and is expensive when well-made, but it is most definitely effective—able to compete with fiberglass and graphite in placement, accuracy, and casting distances when used by an experienced fisherman. Cheaper bamboo rods such as the Orvis Madison or HL Leonard Deluxe, start at around $600. You will have to pay about this much to get a bamboo rod of any degree of trustworthiness—immune to warping, wetness, and ferrule loosening and corrosion. Orvis Battenkills run around $775, and offer fine quality and workmanship, though the rod material may be somewhat flawed in appearance; Thomas & Thomas, Winston, and Ron Kusse make quality bamboo rods in the $700 to $800 price range.

Graphite

Thanks again, NASA. From America's space program came the superlight, superstrong building material: graphite. Graphite rods revolutionized the fly tackle industry and have done more than anything to transform bamboo rods into collector's objects rather than everyday fly rods. The introduction of graphite design has meant that both beginning and expert fly-fishermen can become more consistent and successful fly-casters.

Right: *Tiny streams are the province of the ultra-light fly rod.* **Above:** *Most anglers, after most trout, find an 8- to 9-foot rod suitable.*

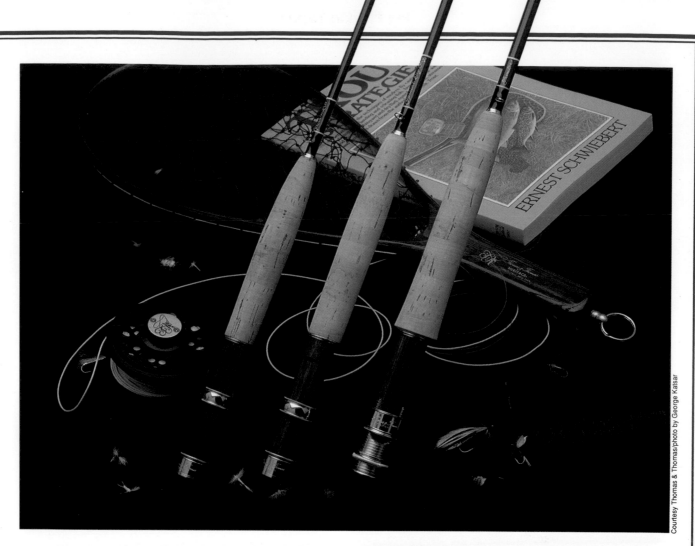

Courtesy Thomas & Thomas/photo by George Katsar

Fly-Rod Checklist

■ A quality rod around 8 to 8½ feet in length should have at least eight line guides, and preferably ten.

■ The guide windings should be uniform, well wound, and smooth.

■ Trims should be done with thread, and the alignment of the windings should be neat and straight.

■ The fly-rod blank (the base material from which the rod is made) should be free of surface imperfections.

■ The cork on the handle and reel seat should be smooth, slightly pitted cork; lower-quality rod handles are often wrapped with pocked, blemished cork.

Courtesy Thomas & Thomas/photo by George Katsar

Graphite offers advantages in modulus elasticity (the degree to which it resists bending), damping (the rate at which the wiggle of the rod tip dies out after a cast), and weight—all of which translate to more casting power and control. Graphite's combination of stiffness and sensitivity provides the fly-fisherman with the opportunity to cast to large fish with small flies tied on very fine, very light leaders. Graphite falls short of fiberglass in sheer tensile strength.[26]

When shopping for a graphite rod, remember a few things. One, no rod is made from pure graphite. Even the best Orvis graphite rods are about 95-percent grapite. Don't trust any rod labeled 100-percent graphite. Second, since graphite has a high modulus of elasticity—it is a very stiff material—make sure that you're not buying an over-snappy stick that will shoot your line across the creek like an arrow. Check the rod's tapering with the store clerk. The graphite rod needs to be finely tapered; poor or insufficient tapering leads to over-stiff rods.

You will get more rod-for-the-money with graphite. Graphite rods weigh much less than bamboo, while offering better kick, better range, more backbone, and a better feel.

Fiberglass

Some rod-makers build wonderful fly rods with fiberglass, but graphite is threatening the role of fiberglass in the building of quality fly rods today. Fiberglass is lighter than bamboo, but heavier than graphite. Graphite rods of similar quality can be the same price as quality fiberglass rods. Unfortunately for fiberglass fly-rod makers everywhere, graphite simply out-performs fiberglass for the money. You can pay $200 for a good fiberglass rod, but a comparable graphite rod can be had for the same money, offering more power and sensitivity at a lighter weight.

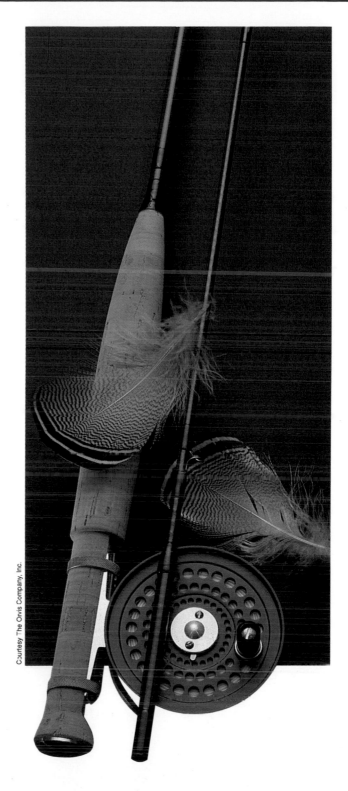

Courtesy The Orvis Company, Inc.

Top Left: *Note the beautiful cherry wood reel seats on these T&T graphite fly rods.*
Bottom Left: *Smooth, slightly pitted cork on the handle is one sign of a well-made fly rod (T&T graphite).*

Above: *Graphite's combination of stiffness and sensitivity provides the fly-angler with the opportunity to cast to large fish with small flies tied on very fine leaders. No one makes better graphite rods than Orvis.*

REELS

Unlike other reels, the fly reel's primary function is storing line. Except for larger trout, the fly reel is not critical in landing a fish, and is never involved in casting. While purchasing a reel for your fly rod is not as crucial to fly-fishing success as the proper selection of the rod itself, money spent on an unreliable, poorly-made reel, or a reel ill-matched to your fly rod, is money wasted. If you buy a cheap reel, sooner or later (and probably sooner) you'll have to replace that gum-ball-machine model with the real McCoy.

Cheap reels fall apart. Anyone who expects to fight large trout must be aware that the fish will fight long and hard, stripping off hundreds of feet of line, and straining reel components. Cheap reels often cannot handle this sort of action. Don't ruin one of the peak experiences of your fly-fishing life with a cheap reel that might blow off the rod. Finally, get a quality reel because quality reels are wonderful things to own, to hold, and to see. Their parts are exquisitely fitted, the handle turns with lovely ease. The heft of their weight, the gloss of their finish, and the feel of their parts adds an element of quality to your sporting life that is deeply satisfying; it is for satisfactions like these that one goes fly-fishing.

What makes a good fly-fishing reel? Let's start with the reel capacity—the amount of fly line and "backing" (the braided line wound on the reel and tied to the fly line that gives the fishermen extra line if a fish makes a long run). Every reel should offer enough room for 50 to 75 yards of backing and the right amount of fly line.

Better reels offer proper line capacity. Fighting bigger fish requires a good deal of heavy line. Generally, 75 to 100 yards of 4-weight line is all the light angler needs; 150 to 160 yards of 8-weight is sufficient for heavy freshwater angling, while saltwater fishermen should load about 300 to 350 yards of 9- to 11-weight line on their reels.

Good reels are made with light materials; however, it is just as important that the weight of your reel matches the rod weight and provides the right balance and heft. The better reels for freshwater trout fishing weigh between 2½ and 6 ounces, with some exceptions. Saltwater, steelhead, and salmon reels will weigh in the 9- to 12-ounce range.

Examine the reel-drag system. Reels use a number of different drag systems. ("Drag" is the mechanical function that creates friction on the reel as a fish is pulling off line.) In knob-adjusted drag, triangular-shaped pawls slow the reel spool through spring-loaded

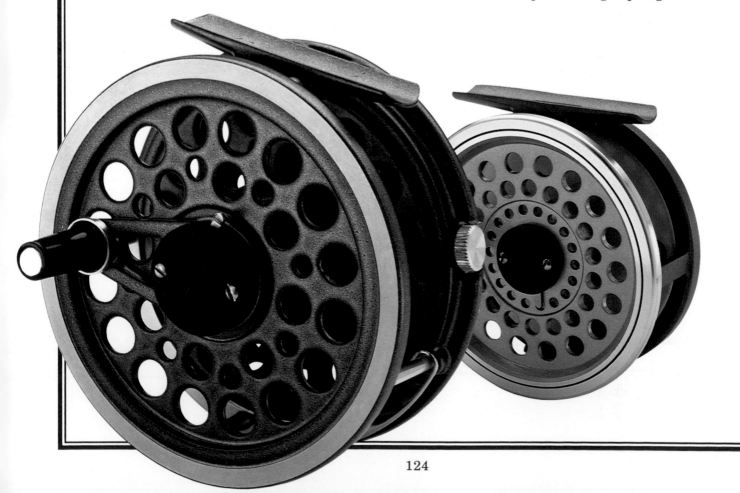

Courtesy The Orvis Company, Inc.

Fly-Reel Checklist

◻ There should be no play between clicks in the drag system. Under steady pressure, the spool should turn one click at a time. The drag clicks and drag system should look, feel, and sound both tight and solid when working the drag at light and heavy settings.

◻ The reel should be free of imperfections in casting or stamping.

◻ As the handle turns, the gap between spool and frame should remain the same.

◻ The spool release should be made of metal and should click in and out with authority and no looseness or play.

◻ There should be almost no play between the spool shaft and the reel spindle.

Left: *The parts of a fly reel are simple: spool, spool release, drag mechanism, reel seat, and handle. The best fly reels are machined from solid metal stock, but many reliable models are made from stamped metal parts, molded plastic, or graphite. Above: Fly reels are available in a range of sizes and weights.*

tension, which the fisherman adjusts with a knob. Cheaper reels are built with only one pawl, which usually means the drag system will be weak and difficult to adjust. The better reels use two pawls. Top-of-the-line reels feature more sophisticated drag systems, including the palm-check pawl drag and the disc-driven drag system, which is just about indestructible.[28]

Reels are made from stamped metal parts, molded plastic, graphite, or are machined from solid metal stock (aluminum, magnesium, steel, or some combination of these). Generally, least expensive and least reliable reels are built from stamped parts, while the top-of-the-line reels are cut from solid, metal stock; however, you can find terrific reels made with any of these materials.

A gorgeous steelhead from North Santiam River, Oregon

THE TACKLE SHOP

FLY-FISHING RODS

BEST QUALITY

Orvis

The Orvis Company in Manchester, Vermont, looms for many anglers, including this one, as the ultimate bastion of American quality workmanship. It is one of the few corporate names in America truly synonymous with quality—to those who fly-fish and even those who do not. Ask a friend about Orvis—chances are they will know at least this: Orvis makes the best.

The Orvis fly rod is a product of slow, painstaking, handmade craft that, time and again, out-performs the competition. Orvis has been making rods in their factory since 1856. They are the only company in the world still making all four kinds of fly rods—graphite, boron and graphite, bamboo, and fiberglass—from scratch. In all its graphite rods,

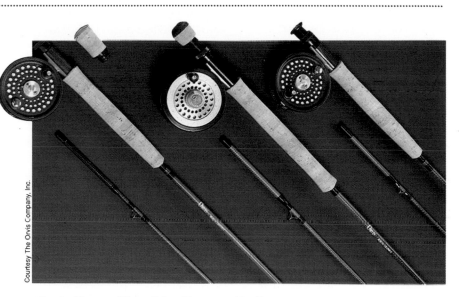

Orvis Boron/Graphite Tarpon Rod

Orvis uses a low modulus (low stiffness) graphite that gives the rod a sweet, easy action and provides the angler with a great deal of control.

Orvis Battenkill Flea Bamboo

This rod is 6½ feet, 2½ ounces of slow-action beauty. An extremely delicate and sensitive

rod of unparalleled response. Around $1,025.

Orvis Boron/Graphite 9 foot, 5½ ounce Light Tarpon

Winner of the 1987 *Rod & Reel* contest for best fishing tackle, fly rod category: The judges called this rod (and the 8-foot 9-inch bonefish rod) "just about

Orvis Battenkill Flea Fly Rod

perfect." In "practiced hands these rods are deadly accurate, powerful-casting, fish-lifting tools." Ceramic guides on the butt section, black, hard anodized-aluminum reel seat. A mighty rod designed to vanquish a mighty fish. Approximately $425.

G. Loomis IMX Series

New graphite technology in IMX rods means that the graphite delivers its well-known "modulus"—or sensitivity—while matching a fiberglass rod in tensile strength. Previously, graphite strength dropped as its modulus increased. Loomis' new rods have maintained sensitivity and added strength. Loomis calls these rods the "fastest dampening, highest performing rods available..." Available in 2- and 3-weights weighing as little as 1¼ ounces, and 4- and 5-weights that never ex-

ceed 3 ounces in weight; the Loomis 5-weight is 9 feet long and weighs 2¾ ounces. Medium steelhead and light saltwater fly rods are also available in the series in 6-, 7-, and 8-weights. This is high performance with a lifetime guarantee. Prices from $275 to $315.

Sage Reserve Power

A hot rod. The Sage graphite RP rod has a more progressive taper than a traditional fly rod, which means the RP's light, sensitive tip comes into power quickly, giving the caster higher line speed, line control, and accuracy. This high-speed, sensitive, lightweight graphite rod casts smoothly and sharply: It is a rod for the casting fanatic. The Sage line is booming in popularity. Sizes range from 7 feet 9 inches to 9 feet, at prices from $240 to $300.

HL Leonard Hunt Series Bamboo

Made with dark, open-flame cane, these are among the world's finest fly rods. Available in eleven different models, prices ranging from $950 to $1,075.

Fenwick World Class

Every Fenwick World Class Fly Rod features HMG III Helical Bias Graphite Construction blanks with tremendous hoop strength that cast smoothly and dampen quickly. The fast settling-down of the rod after the cast gives you better control and accuracy over a wide range of distances. The World Class is available in rod sizes that begin at 3-weight for light saltwater fishing. The 4-weight model weighs in at a deliciously light 3 ounces.

G. Loomis IMX Fly Series

Kusse Bamboo

Handmade by Ron Kusse in upstate New York, these highly popular bamboo rods have definitely been a hit among fly-fishermen. The Bamboo features two tips, select cherry-wood reel seats, jewelry-grade nickel silver fittings, and Super Z ferrules. This beauty costs about $700.

B E S T   V A L U E

CRI
(Catskill Research Incorporated, distributed by Cortland Line Company)

CRI pride themselves as the wizards of graphite, and it is not an undeserved self-image. The CRI fly rod is Catskill Research's best rod. Its exceptional thinness, flex, crisp response, smooth casting power, and beautifully delicate parabolic action are the result of its "30-T aircraft carbon graphite cloth construction." This exclusive process allows for thinner construction with unequalled "united solidity."

The CRI rod is 98-percent graphite cloth, a remarkably high ratio. This is a high performance rod that packs explosive casting power for the price. Reasonable prices begin at $84.

Pflueger Medalist

The Medalist series is designed specifically for the value-conscious intermediate and advanced fly-fisherman who needs medium-fast action, snappy line speed, and pinpoint control. Good fiberglass construction. Reel seats are wood, individually sanded and coated. Rods range from 3- to 9-weight, at prices from around $80 to $90.

Orvis Deschutes Fly Rod

Cabela's Gary Borger Spectrum Series

Reasonably-priced, high performance rods largely for fly-fishing in the Western United States and Canada. The rods in the series combine delicacy of presentation with reserve power to help the angler throw long casts. These rods are made of IM6 graphite (see Loomis series) but are not the equal of Loomis rods in every performance category. These are extremely smooth-loading and flexing rods that cast with exceptional grace. Pewter-finished reel seats, super-hard stripping, running guides, and flat charcoal finish. Model 3.5, for 3- and 4-weight line, is designed for gentle presentation of large flies on small leaders to large fish, and retails for about $170. Model 5.5, for 5- and 6-weight lines, is an all-around rod for a variety of fly-fishing situations for about $170. Model 7.5, 9.5, and 11.5 are built for steel-head, salmon and big bass, and tarpon-sized saltwater game, respectively, for prices starting around $220.

Orvis 9-Foot Western Series "Deschutes"

This 4 ounce rod can perform a great number of fly-casting tasks—long, short into the wind, and roll casts—with stunning ease. Popular in the Northwest and the Rockies, this is a pefect all-around rod for the Western fly-fishermen. Priced at around $275.

Fenwick Eagle

Reliable Fenwick quality at a reasonable price. Fenwick's chief rod designer, Jim Green, has built in some high-rent features on this low-priced fiberglass fly rod. The reel seats and stripper guides are made of aluminum, and the snake guides are hard chrome. It is a nicely balanced rod that is designed for rookies, with few features and, of course, fiberglass construction. Orvis offers cheaper rods of comparable quality, but Fenwick is still a fly rod worth investigating for the beginner. The Fenwick Eagle will cost the careful shopper between $70 and $80.

LIGHT 2-WEIGHT FLY RODS

Thomas and Thomas Whisper Lite 7-foot

Fine, delicate rod. Casts a 3-weight line. Ideal for precision fishing of dry flies for flighty, nervous Eastern trout on small, intimate, wind-protected streams.

Orvis 8'6"
Western Series

This fast-action whippy rod offers all the action you can find in a 2-weight rod. Fish with this rod even in windy conditions and for long distances. This is a tough 2-weight that acts like a bigger rod.

REELS

BEST QUALITY

Hardy Perfect Series

The English first introduced the Hardy reel in 1891—quite a pedigree. Hardy Perfect reels are made from heavy-duty aluminum alloy, machined to close tolerances and fitted with stainless steel ball bearings, making them nearly frictionless. They have a quick-release spool and a compensating click drag. Weights range from 5¾ to 8½ ounces in prices from $100 to $140.

Cortland CRI

The spool and frame of this reel are hand-honed from a single block of aluminum. The adjustable clutch-drag mechanism is guaranteed for life and has an easy right-left conversion. These lightweight reels weigh in at 2.7 ounces for freshwater reels and 4.8 ounces for saltwater models. Prices begin at about $125 and range to over $150.

Fin Nor

Among the finest fly reels ever made. Available in direct-drive and anti-reverse models, which offer the highest strength, balance, and lightness possible in fly-reel construction. Both incorporate large-diameter, brake-disc drag systems. The four standard models are direct drive, which means the handle turns as the line runs out. The two anti-reverse models allow the handle to remain stationary as the fish runs. Direct-drive reels come in four models—the smallest holding 150 yards of 7-weight line and the largest holding 300 yards of 12-weight line. The anti-reverse comes in four models at identical capacities. Prices from $180 and up.

Orvis CFO

This is the highest expression of the Orvis art in reel manufacture. The four CFO freshwater reel models are cast from aluminum alloy. They are very strong and very light. The CFO II weighs just 2 ounces, while the CFO III weighs 3¼ ounces. Both are terrific all-around fly reels. On every CFO model, the spool rim is exposed for easy palming and control of long-running salmon, trout, and steelhead. The CFO reel is fitted with an adjustable drag system and nickel silver line guard. The CFO, however, is *not* designed for saltwater fishing. The CFO weighs about 3½ ounces, and the CFO V weighs 4¼ ounces. $140.

Orvis Western Fly Rod Series

Scientific Angler System Two Fly Reels

Fenwick World Class

This innovative reel has high-quality features that include: two individual settings for click tension and drag; a left-right conversion option; leverage-adjustment reel control knob; and a special drag that eliminates spool overruns. Prices range from $110 to over $200 for saltwater model (12 ounces). Freshwater reels tip the scale at 4 ounces in their lightest weight.

Ross RR

Destined to be a classic of American craftsmanship. Ross Hauck guarantees his work in writing to its original owner. He machines each reel from a 3-pound block of aluminum-bar stock that has been rolled under tremendous pressure to give it a grain very close to wood. The finished reel is beautiful to behold and built to extremely exact tolerances. The Ross "S" is the saltwater version. Prices begin at $150.

BEST VALUE
Berkley Specialist

Berkley delivers quality fly reels at lower prices than a good deal of the competition. Cut from corrosion-resistant aluminum, each reel is fitted with pop-off graphite spool, three-position drag clicker, and palming drag. While not made of graphite, the Berkley reels boast excellent workmanship for the price and are guaranteed by Berkley. The smallest reel (2.9 ounces) can be had for around $30, though prices can run higher than $40.

Scientific Angler System One

This reel is built from cast aluminum alloy with a durable, baked-enamel finish. The adjustable click drag and exposed spool rim provide a good measure of fish-fighting control. Quick-reverse spools. Approximately $75.

Cortland LTD Graphite

Superlight graphite construction, with the lightest model weighing in at 3 ounces, and the 12-weight reel weighing just 4¾ ounces! Very competitive pricing at $55 and up.

Orvis Battenkill

This is the Orvis fly-fishing reel that offers the most to the fly-fisherman. Not their cheapest reel, though far from the most expensive, the Battenkill offers quality and reliable workmanship in a reel designed with the features important to most past-the-beginning stage fly anglers. Two Battenkill models feature desirable Teflon disc drag, which is important in landing strong, acrobatic fish. All three of the Battenkill reel models are built with counter-weighted spools, anodized aluminum, and stainless steel internal parts for corrosion resistance. Batenkill 5/6: weighs 4 ounces and has a diameter of 3⅛ inches. Batenkill 7/8: weighs 4½ ounces and has a diameter of 3⅜ inches. Batenkill 8/9: Weighs 4¾ ounces and has a diameter of 3⅜ inches. Reels are available at prices ranging from about $75 to $90.

Valentine

These reels come from a small manufacturer in Massachusetts. The reels are built first and foremost for durability. All parts are stamped from solid aluminum, which gives the reel more strength. But remember, this is a workhorse reel for workhorse fly-fishermen who spend a lot of time fishing, and fishing with success. For example, the Valentine boasts a super-powerful disc drag that is strong enough to stop a train. The spools are counterbalanced to provide stability and strength during long, hard fights with big browns or steelheads. The Valentine reel weighs more than comparably priced models, and may feel uncomfortable on a light graphite rod. This is not the reel for anglers who are putting together an ultra light outfit. Prices for Valentines begin at around $80.

BEST FOR THE BEGINNER

JW Young

Super value for an English fly reel. Dual click adjustable drag with quick release spool. From $25 to $30.

Martin "Fly Wate" Series

For big fish. Made from lightweight aluminum alloy and equipped with coil-spring adjustable drags. The coil-spring powered pawl drag is "cammed" to allow for settings from light to heavy. Easy right-left conversion. Each reel has twin line guides and push-button release. All models weigh from 5¼ to 10 ounces and cost less than $30.

Martin "Tuffy" Series

Made from anodized aluminum alloy, with on-off clicks. This series is built without adjustable drag and is designed for small-trout fishing. A good beginner's reel starting at $20.

Pflueger Medalist

These trusty workhorses are a fine buy. Nothing fancy, but fly reels are not fancy mechanisms. Aluminum frame and spool, spool release, and fully adjustable drag. Prices start at $28 for a 4-ounce reel and range to $80 for the 13-ounce, saltwater reel.

Courtesy Valentine Fly Reels/Val-Craft Inc.

Valentine Fly Reels offer indestructible drag systems.

Fly Lines And Leaders

The beginning fly-fishermen will find that an extraordinary amount of technology surrounds the construction and use of fly line. Technical developments over the last 30 years have multiplied the options available to the fly-fisherman. This is with good reason. The fly line actually delivers the fly to the water and determines in part how deeply that fly will be positioned in the water.

Choosing leaders, while less complicated, still requires a slightly refined knowledge of fly-fishing terms and stream conditions. The beginning fly-fisherman is wise to remember the importance of fly line to hooking and landing trout. The great Lee Wulff, in his book TROUT ON A FLY, wrote: "Line is the most important part of fly-fishing tackle. Back in 1941, when I was pioneering the taking of big salmon on featherweight rods, there were many statements made that there was a certain minimum rod length and strength required to take a salmon. I decided to settle the argument, and by casting by hand without a rod, I hooked a ten-pound Atlantic salmon and played it directly from the reel, which I held in one hand while reeling with the other.... It established the importance of the line."

FLY-LINE SPECIFICATIONS

Fly lines are discussed with a peculiar vernacular that describes their various characteristics and indicate to the experienced fisherman how that particular line will perform. Here are definitions of some of these terms, and explanations of how to figure out what each particular fly line offers.

TAPER

The taper of fly line for the most part, controls the two variables of casting: distance and accuracy. Level lines are built with no taper, and have been entirely outmoded by new designs. A level line, while cheap, is virtually impossible to cast with any distance or accuracy.

Double-taper fly line is tapered at either end of the fly line and is perfectly symmetrical. The tapered front end gives the angler great line control and casting accuracy. The double-taper fly is best for small stream and dry-fly casting. But because the weight of the fly line is distributed evenly, and not at the end of the fly line, double-taper line does not cast as far as weight-forward taper.

Floating double-taper line is the best purchase for beginning fly-fishermen. It allows great accuracy and most of the casting distance beginners need.

Many long-distance casters—lake fly-fishermen, salmon and steelhead fishermen—prefer **weight-forward taper** fly line. This fly line moves most of the line weight up front, with a relatively heavy front section of line tapering to a thin diameter at the middle and back. Weight-forward taper allows the angler to cast much farther and with greater power. This means the fly-fisherman can reach more distant feeding trout with one or two quick casts rather than with a series of back casts.[29]

Shooting taper is similar to weight-forward line except that the heavier, weighted-front section of line is attached to monofilament or backing line, allowing the fly-fisherman to make the longest casts possible with a fly rod. With all the fly-line weight up front, the caster can "shoot" amazingly long casts. This especially serves the saltwater and flats fly-fishermen who need to quickly reach fast-moving tarpon, permit, and bonefish with long, fast casts.

FLY-LINE WEIGHT

This specification tells the fly-fisherman how the first 30 feet of the fly line weighs. Lines in the 10- to 12-weight class are suitable for big freshwater trout and salmon. Line weights in the 8- to 10-weight class are best for stalking the bigger trout of the West and Great Lakes. Line in the 4- to 8-weight class are best for all-around small stream and river trout fishing.

The weight of your fly line determines the rest of your tackle selections—from rod, to reel, to fly. The size of the fly you choose must match the line on your reel, and the line on your reel must match the weight range of the fly rod. This is why fly-fishermen of any experience carry extra reel spools strung with different weight line. Heavier flies must be cast on heavier-line weights. However, it does all tend to work out in the field. If you're fishing for little browns in the Catskills, no doubt you will be casting smaller flies. And you will be using a lighter line weight and rod because you don't need the power of a big rod for small rivers and streams.

FLY-LINE GRAVITY

Fly-line gravity tells the fisherman whether a particular fly line sinks, floats, or both. Floating fly line is used for dry-fly fishing,

and some wet-fly fishing. In some wet-fly fishing (wet flies sink, dry flies float), floating line allows the angler to see the strike or "take" of his wet fly or nymph, much as a bobber does for the bait-fisherman.

Floating/sink tip lines build a sinking tip onto a floating fly line that allows the fly or nymph to be fished at a medium water depth while still allowing the fisherman to observe his line.

Intermediate sinking lines drift below the surface of the water a few inches over the length of the line. Intermediate lines never sink more than a few inches, which means that sink tip lines almost always work better in any situation where you want to fish a fly a few inches under the surface. This is because the fisherman has the added advantage of watching his line.

Sinking lines sink. Period. Some sink deeper than others, and some sink very deep. Most line makers will list on the box the sink rate in inches per second. Deep sinking lines are employed on lakes, deep rivers, in saltwater for salmon, and the saltwater flats for tarpon and bonefish.

Now, let's head into the tackle shop to look at some fly line brands at different price levels. Remember that fly lines are available in many colors, and you should choose the color easiest for you to see. Most fly-fishing experts have stated that trout see fly line cast on the water as a dark line in the surface film, no matter what the color. You'll have to make this decision for yourself. Bright green or orange line will be easier to spot early and late in the day when the sun is low.

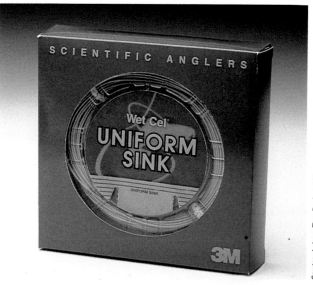

Fly Sizes and Line Weights

Line Weight	Range of Fly Sizes
3	16 to 28
4	14 to 26
5	12 to 22
6	8 to 20
7	6 to 16
8	4 to 14
9	1/0 to 10
10	3/0 to 8
11	4/0 to 4
12	6/0 to 1/0

Dry-fly fishing usually requires flies in the 12 to 28 size. So, when you decide what kind of fishing you'll be doing, decide on a line weight, and a rod and reel to match.

The most popular fly line is the floating variety, since most fly-fishermen prefer to catch trout on the surface—if they have a choice— where hatches, takes, presentation, and strikes can be observed.

Fly-line Codes

Figuring out just what kind of fly line you're buying can be daunting. Fly-line boxes have more numbers and codes on them than a computer software program. But, as in everything with fly fishing, the system is not as complicated as it looks. All fly line is marked with a code on the container. This code gives you all the specifications of the fly line. Let's take a look at a sample code:

ST8F/S

The code breaks down this way:

ST: Shooting
8: taper line weight
F/S: floating line and sinking tip

So, the floating fly line here has a shooting taper with a line weight of 8, and a sinking tip for fishing wet flies just below the water's surface. This fly line would be well suited to fishing wet flies for cutthroat trout in broad, fast moving mountain streams like the Madison in Yellowstone Park.

The other specifications are coded this way:

L: level
DT: double taper
ST: shooting taper

F: floating
I: intermediate sinking
S: sinking

The middle part of the code always designates line weight.

THE TACKLE SHOP

The few fly lines we've selected here represent types of fly line of differing quality and, thus, differing prices.

Cortland, Scientific Angler, and Orvis are generally regarded by expert fly-fishermen and tackle dealers as the best manufacturers of fly lines in America.

LINES

BEST QUALITY

Cortland 444

Regarded as the world's finest floating, nylon-tapered fly line. A new chemical in the fly line's finish, combined with a special, tubular braided center, makes this a superb custom-crafted line. Delicate balance. Peach color. Prices for the WF and DT are both approximately $28.

Cortland 444SL

Cortland's latest, most highly rated fly line offers a balance of suppleness for casting accuracy, and stiffness for casting distance. Unique finish builds stiffness while retaining feel.

A perfect line for long, controlled casts. Both the DT and WF are about $32.

Cortland 444 Sink Tip

The heavy tip sinks, and wet flies and nymphs drift to the middle of the current, while the balance of the line floats high for easy sighting. Peach colored except for darker-hued sinking tip. Both the DT and WF are about $28.

Lee Wulff's Triangle Taper Fly Line

This heavy 9-weight is ideal for Atlantic salmon, steelhead, and big trout. This model joins other Triangle Taper weights, in a group of delicate lines that offer superb roll-casting capability. These weight-forward lines are white for easy visibility. From about $34.

Lee Wulff's Long Belly

Combines the advantages of both double-tapered and weight-forward line, offers casting control and momentum for long-distance casting. From about $34.

Orvis SSS Hy Flote Saltwater

Designed for durability in the hot sun and saltwater, the SSS is coated with a special finish for maximum wear. A shorter front taper increases line momentum, making it easier to cast large flies long distances. About $40.

Lee Wulff Triangle Taper Fly Line

Scientific Angler

Scientific Angler introduced air cell technology to fly lines. Their fly line is made of a special plastic that traps millions of microscopic air bubbles within its Kevlar core. The line is coated with a durable plastic that resists breaking and cracking. Because the fly lines are manufactured under many tons of pressure, the Kevlar core and special polymer coatings are fully integrated. The Scientific Angler lines come in different levels of quality: Ultra, Supreme, and Concept.

Courtesy The Orvis Company, Inc.

Orvis Front Loop Hy Flote

Durable, high-floating fly line coated with a special material that actually repels water and allows line to ride high on the water's surface. Bright yellow color. $34

Orvis Sinking Tip Fly Lines

BEST VALUE

Scientific Angler Shooting Tapers

Sinking: Wet Cell Intermediate I & II—$32.
Weight Forward Hi speed Hi-D Wet Tip—$26.
Air Cell Supreme Floating—$20.

Scientific Angler Wet Cell Full Sinking—$18.

Wet Cell II—$22.
Wet Cell Hi-D Extra Fast sinking—$18.

Orvis Sinking Tip Fly Lines

Double-taper floating line with a 10-foot fast sinking tip that gets nymphs and wet flies down to the big ones. Priced at around $30.

BEST FOR BEGINNERS

Scientific Angler Concept

Concept lines are designed with a special taper that helps counteract common casting problems. Each line is 57 feet long—long enough for the situations most beginning fly-fishermen will encounter. Concept is available in weight-foward, double-taper, and level tapers, in 5 through 8 weights. Priced at around $15.

Cortland Fairplay Fly Lines

For the starting fly-fisherman, available in floating double-taper, floating rocket taper, and level taper. About $15.

Scientific Angler Fly Line Series for salt and freshwater

LEADERS

The leader is the final link between the fly-fisherman and his quarry. The varieties of leaders are not as imposing as fly lines. However, the successful fly-fisherman still must understand what is available, and which leaders work best in different settings.

Leaders come in two basic forms: knotted and continuous taper. Knotted leaders consist of sections of tapered line knotted together during manufacture. Taper allows leaders to uncoil and straighten during the cast: the heavy butt end flips over the light tippet to lightly drop the fly on the water. This ensures quiet, accurate presentation. Knotted leaders are created with extremely precise tapers. The knots make it easy for the angler to tell which end of the leader forms the narrowest taper (where the flies are tied), and to know exactly what the leader dimensions are. Does the length of the butt balance the length of the tippet? How does the butt compare in length in the mid-section? A balanced leader is crucial to successful casting. The fly-fisherman laying a Cream Variant on a pool in the Neversink needs a leader not only perfectly matched to the size of his fly, but one that is balanced in graduation, with the butt end composing about sixty percent of the leader. The graduated, pre-tippet section should use another twenty percent, and the final, finely drawn tippet section should take around twenty percent. This means a good cast will unfurl the leader to set a dry fly as softly as possible on its hackle points.

However, knotted tapers are nowhere near as popular or as well-regarded as continuous tapers. Continuous leaders narrow uniformly, and it takes a sharp eye to find the very end of a spooled leader. Individually packaged continuous leaders are easier to figure out, of course. As each fly is snipped off and changed, the fisherman moves up his leader where the monofilament is thicker, harder to tie, and likely to impede accurate presentation. However, continuous taper leaders offer several advantages. Since the line is not hitched together with knots, it is stronger. Monofilament line wears out where it is knotted. In weedy water, knots can catch on floating leaves and weeds. Continuous taper leaders are less noticeable to trout, since there are no knots to cast a shadow.

Courtesy Leisure Time Products/3M

Leaders are generally 7½ to 9 feet long. In shallow water, where trout are usually skittish, or whenever trout seem visibly spooked by the slightest indication of the fisherman's presence, longer leaders of 9 to 11 feet will make the least possible disturbance. In faster water and deep pools, stick to 9-foot leaders. Shorter, 7½-foot leaders fill the bill for wet fly and nymph fishing or for fast water fly-fishing situations where the sight of the fly line is obscured.

The tippet is the end of the leader where the angler ties the fly. The "x" number on leader packages indicates tippet size—with "x" sizes running from 0x to 8x and 01x to 013x in larger big-water tippets. Higher "x" numbers usually indicate smaller tippets. Most fly-fishermen can handle any fishing situation with leaders sized between 2x and 6x. The smaller leaders are so fine and delicate that great care is required in casting, presentation, and landing, to avoid breaking off flies and fish.

The next table will help you match the right sized leader to the size of the flies you are using. Many fly-fishermen use the "rule-of-4" as a guide. Take the size of your fly, and divide it by 4. This is the largest tippet you should use. If you're fishing with a number 12 fly, for instance, use a 3X or finer tippet between the fly and the line.[31]

Combine this table with the fly line and fly-size table on page 000 to design perfectly balanced fly tackle. Most beginning fly-fishermen want to know what the "test" of leaders are—that is, their tenacity of breaking strength. The strength of leaders depends on the quality of the resin formulation used in the monofilament extrusion process. In other words, factory differences affect leaders as they affect all manufactured

goods. But fly-fishing anglers can search out the strongest leader material by comparing the pound "test" for various diameters labeled on the different leader brands, and choosing the *highest strength per diameter.* A spool of 5x would be considered stronger if it tests at 4.0 pounds than another brand marked 5x at 3.0 pounds.

Climax and Aeon, among other brands, offer the highest test strength per diameter.

No way exists of discovering the best leaders for the fishing you wish to do, except practice and experience. Generally, if you need thicker, stronger leaders to complete long casts and fight bigger fish, try to get them stiff. If you need supple, whippy leaders to chase smaller trout in smaller streams, look for a thin leader—one that is sensitive to wrist action and casting motion.

But just as limp monofilament can stretch too much, giving fish too much leverage against the line, so it is with some of the thinner fly leaders. And stiff leaders—meant to cast large flies—can resist accurate casting. The leaders we list in the tackle shop are generally well-balanced. But, finding leaders of such specific satisfaction takes time. Be patient and keep trying new models.

Top: *In rougher, turbulent, or white water, the fly angler can use shorter leaders which provides better control and easier casting.* Above: *Just as fly lines are designed to float or sink to reach trout at various depths, so it is with leaders.*

© Dave Wonderlich/Dembinsky Photo Assoc.

© Ellie Dietrich

© Dave Wonderlich/Dembinsky Photo Assoc.

© Dick Dietrich

© Greg L. Ryan

© Carl R. Sams II/Dembinsky Photo Assoc.

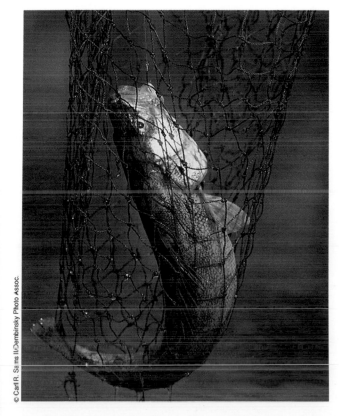

Counter-clockwise from above: *Casting for trout in Pine River, Minnesota. A perfect roll cast in mid-flight. Fishing Tonto Creek at Bear Flat. A significant trout has taken this angler's dry fly. Rainbow trout love fast water. Here an angler lands one on the Gibbon River in Wyoming.*

THE TACKLE SHOP

LEADERS

BEST QUALITY

Aeon Knotless Tapered Leaders

These leaders offer strong tip-pets and a lot of muscle for their diameter. The .011 0x Aeon leader pulls 10-pound test versus 6-pound test for the same diameter Berkley leader. Both the 7½-and 9-foot leaders are about $1.40 each.

Dai-Riki

This new leader from River Run Imports in Montana won the *Rod & Reel Magazine's* "New Products Award" in 1987. About $3.00 per spool.

Orvis Braided Leaders

These leaders offer a 6-foot braided butt and long (60") ta-pered tippet. The Orvis braided leader offers advantages in suppleness, casting efficiency, stretchiness for shock absorp-tion, and easy storage. Tip-top quality at tip-top prices: 9-foot leaders are $8 or more apiece. Looped ends for easy line-leader connection.

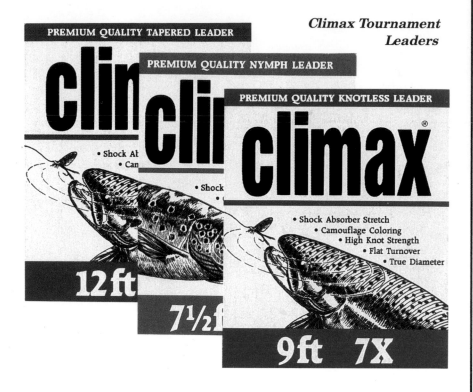

Climax Tournament Leaders

PREMIUM QUALITY TAPERED LEADER

PREMIUM QUALITY NYMPH LEADER

PREMIUM QUALITY KNOTLESS LEADER

climax®

• Shock Absorber Stretch
• Camouflage Coloring
• High Knot Strength
• Flat Turnover
• True Diameter

12 ft

7½f

9ft 7X

BEST VALUE

Berkley Specialist Knotless "Not a Knot" Tapered leaders.

Traditional configuration ta-pered leaders for all fly lines and all fly-fishing conditions. The 7½-foot leaders are about $.95, and the 9-foot leaders are about $1. They range from 0x to 6x.

Umpqua Tapered Leaders

Easy turnover and high-strength monofilament, 0x to 6x sizes at around $2.00 each.

Climax Tournament Leaders

Exceptionally fine tapers make Climax leaders the industry standard in "turning over" dry flies for perfect presentations. Super-high density means that Climax leaders are stronger at each "x" size than most of the competition.

A real value. Prices range from $1.85 and up for leaders in lengths from 7½ to 15 feet for various kinds of fishing (saltwater, big-game, steel-head, salmon, and small trout), and are available in sizes from 0x to 7x.

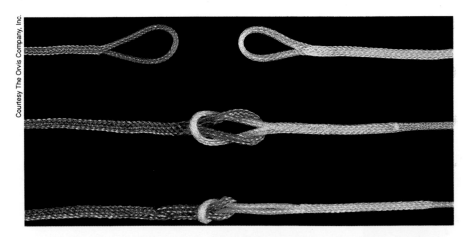

Courtesy The Orvis Company, Inc.

Orvis' Leader Loops makes changing leaders a knotless task

Scientific Anglers System Two Leaders

Cortland Precision 1 Leaders

These 7½-, 9-, and 12-foot dry-fly leaders are very stretchy, which means good shock resistance. Coated with a unique non-glare camouflage finish. About $1.70 each.

BEST FOR THE BEGINNER

Maxima Leader Material

Low-cost leaders that can still be depended on to withstand small and medium fish strikes, and turn over small and medium flies, but the leader is too soft for larger flies. In sizes from 1x to 013x, priced at about $1.75 per spool.

Berkley Specialist "Not A Knot" Leaders

A SHOWCASE OF VINTAGE TROUT AND SALMON FLIES

There are two main categories of flies: specifics and attractors. *Specifics* match as closely as possible particular insect forms. *Attractors* suggest no particular species of insect, but draw the trout's attention through a combination of color and movement suggestive of a range of insect foods (there are also minnow attractors). The flies we've listed here are either specifics or attractors and are distinguished by their widespread popularity among working fly-fishermen, and their recognition in the fly-fishing press and literature.

The flies in our collection are also distinguished by their American pedigree: All were first tied for American streams, rivers, and lakes. Dry flies imitate hatching aquatic insects and float on the surface, and those we have chosen here imitate the major American stream hatches. Wet flies imitate or suggest a variety of insects in subaquatic environments, or minnows. Streamers are minnow imitations; terrestrials suggest earth bound insects, like grasshoppers and

ants, that are blown into streams and gulped by trout; nymphs imitate the tasty larval forms of various aquatic insects.

TERRESTRIALS

Letort Cricket

Invented by Ernest Schwiebert, Edward Shank, and Edward Koch. This fly was first tested on the Letort River, in Letort, Pennsylvania.[32]

Black Ant

This fly can be tied in a number of ways, including the version shown here, which uses two cells of black foam.

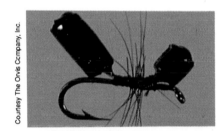

Courtesy The Orvis Company, Inc.

Orvis Black Ant

DRY FLIES

Hendrickson

Represents the female of Ephemerella subvaria, a major early spring hatch. The Hendrickson was invented by Roy Steenrod of Liberty, New York.[33]

Red Quill

Imitates the female of Ephemeridae subvaria. The Red Quill dry fly was invented by the genius of matching the hatch, Art Flick.[34]

Light Cahill

Invented by Theodore Gordon and refined by William Chandler of Neversink, New York. This fly imitates the major late spring hatch of Stenonema Canadensis.[35]

Pale Evening Dun

Another great Catskills and Vermont fly that has caught thousands of fish.

Courtesy Thomas & Thomas/photo by H. Norvel

Dark Henderson　　　　**Red Quill**　　　　**March Brown**

Light Cahill

Adams

Quill Gordon

Blue Wing Sulphur Dun

Cream Variant

Represents Potamanthus distinctus, the last large mayfly to appear on Eastern streams in the spring.

Quill Gordon Dry

Iron Fraudator imitation. First tied around the turn of the century by Theodore Gordon, the father of American fly-fishing.

Blue Wing Sulphur Dun

Created by Vincent Marinaro of Harrisburg, Pennsylvania in the early 1930s. Imitates the many pale-yellow sulphur-fly varieties.

Pale Evening Dun

To quote Ray Bergman's classic, TROUT: "This pattern, as far as I know, sort of grew out of correspondence between Charlie Fox, of Harrisburg and New Cumberland, Pennsylvania, and the writer, over a number of years. Its usefulness is in no way confined to the Pennsylvania streams. No matter where you are, if sulphury flies hatch, this one might do the trick."[37]

Adams

Originated by Len Halladay and christened on the river Boardman in 1922. It was named after Charles F. Adams of Ohio, the first to use it, and he reported its success to Halladay. The Adams is the most popular dry fly in America.

American March Brown

Stenonema Vicarium imitation. First tied by Preston Jennings, author of one of the most important early books on angling etomology, A BOOK OF TROUT FLIES (1935), which systematically organizes

Hendrickson

American fly-fishing patterns, and their relationship to insect hatches.[36]

W E T   F L I E S

Dave's Sculpin

From David Whitlock, who first tested it on the White River in Arkansas.

Zug Bug

This imitates a variety of related subaquatic insects. Western fly-fishing favorite.

Wooly Worm

This sinking nymph has been hauling in champion trout around Montana and the Rockies since it was first cast around 1933. Invented by Dan Martinez, the wooly worm is part mayfly nymph, part caterpillar, and one of the most effective wet flies ever tied.

Gray Ghost

Black Wooly Worm

Courtesy Cabela's

S T R E A M E R S

Muddler Minnow

Dan Gapen of Minnesota popularized and streamlined the use of this universally popular streamer. Gapen developed the present-day Muddler Minnow during the late 1930s on the Nipigon River in Ontario, Canada, where he caught dozens of large, trophy trout with variations of the Muddler.

White Marabou

First tied by AM Ballou of North Dighton, Massachusetts. A magnificent fly that draws curious trout out from under cover.

Gray Ghost

On July 1, 1924, a Maine housewife named Carrie Gertrude Stevens tied what would become one of the most successful streamers ever tied, the Gray Ghost. This smelt-imitating streamer is enormously effective. The state of Maine erected a plaque honor-

Courtesy Thomas & Thomas/photo by H. Norvel

Cream Variant

ing Ms. Stevens and her invention, at the site of her home. It reads: "Fishermen: Pause here a moment and pay your respects to Carrie Gertrude Stevens. On July 1, 1924, while engaged in household tasks in her home across this portage road, she was inspired to create a new fish fly pattern. With housework abandoned, her nimble hands had soon completed her vision. In less than an hour the nearby Upper Dam Pool had yielded a 6 pound, 13 ounce brook trout to the new fly that would become known throughout the world as the Gray Ghost."[38]

S A L M O N A N D S T E E L H E A D

Black Bomber

The Bomber series was popularized on the Miramichi River, in Nova Scotia, in 1967.

Black Wulff

Lee Wulff's salmon and trout patterns have become standard patterns for both fish. He developed them on the Ausable River in 1929.

Jock Scott

One of the all time classic salmon flies, but difficult to tie.

S A L T W A T E R

Tarpon Cockroach

Created by John Emery and Norman Duncan. Can be tied up to 10 inches long.

Pink Shrimp

First tied by flats-aficionado Joe Brooks during his pioneering exploration of fly rodding for bonefish around the Florida Keys.

Courtesy The Orvis Company, Inc.

Muddler Minnow

Courtesy The Orvis Company, Inc.

White Marabou

Courtesy Thomas & Thomas/photo by H. Norvel

Pale Evening Dun

Courtesy Cabela's

Zug Bug

Courtesy Cabela's

TYING KITS

Tying flies can be, for many new fly-fishermen, the most intimidating aspect of the sport. To create fish-catching flies out of bits and pieces of feathers, fur, hair, and yarn seems impossibly complicated. But, as with the rest of fly-fishing, the tasks are accomplished by mastering specific principles which can be learned. These tasks range from forming wings to tying bodies, from learning key knots to choosing hooks and correct materials. Beginners should choose one of the many excellent introductory fly-tying books (Eric Leiser's THE COMPLETE BOOK OF FLY TYING [Knopf] is probably the best for the money) and one of the fly-tying kits we list below. Enrolling in a good fly-tying class will cut the time and effort of the learning process, and provide you with a ready-made network of collegial tiers.

Flies are tied from an exotic and even weird assortment of materials that can make the dedicated fly tier seem like a discount Frankenstein. Tiers stockpile fur from the opossum, rabbit, squirrel, moose, elk, antelope, and woodchuck; large hunks of rooster feathers called "hackle"; and feathers from the ostrich, partridge, English grouse, turkey, and peacock. They combine tufts and strands of this stuff with wax, glue, and thread to create beautiful flies, which resemble the bugs and minnows trout love to eat.

One of the satisfactions of fly-fishing is catching a good trout on one of your own flies. The fly-tying process teaches the tier a great deal about the art of matching flies to insects and other aquatic forms.

Above: *Mickey Finn and Marabou.* **Below:** *One of the highest satisfactions in fly-fishing is catching a trout made with one of your own flies.* **Opposite page:** *Orvis Fly Tying Kit offers top-quality tools and materials.*

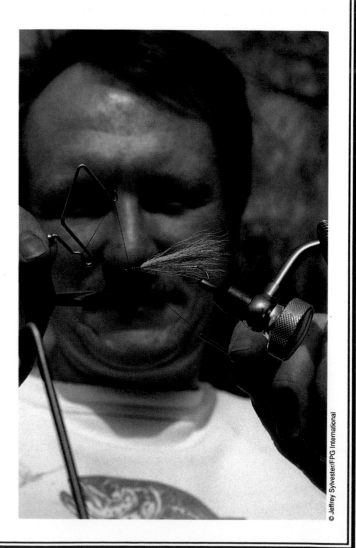

© Jeffrey Sylvester/FPG International

150

THE TACKLE SHOP

FLY-TYING KITS

BEST QUALITY

Crest 300

This top of the line kit contains Crest 300 Supreme vise, stainless bobbin, hackle pliers, 4-inch scissors, bodkin, hair stacker, hooks, dubbing wax, and complete assortment of fly-tying materials. Costs about $70. We highly recommend it.

Thompson Regency Fly-Tying Kit

Includes a Thompson Patriot vise, complete assortment of hooks and materials, non-skid hackle pliers, midge bobbin, bodkin, midge supreme scissors, head cement, basic fly-tying manual. About $65.

Orvis Fly Tying Kit

Learn how to tie dries, wets, streamers, and nymphs, with materials included for all four styles. Top quality materials include hooks, furs, feathers, tinsel, thread, hackle, vise, bodkin, and other tools.

BEST VALUE

Crest 200

Features Crest 200 custom vise, stainless steel bobbin, hackle pliers, scissors, half-hitch/bodkin, hooks, head cement, and an excellent assortment of fly-tying materials. Around $60.

Kauffman's Streamborn Basic Beginner's Kit

This kit is oriented to Western fly-patterns for the stonefly and salmonfly hatches, big rainbows, and steelhead of the Rockies and Northwest. Everything the beginner needs to tie an assortment of the crucial flies and nymphs, including parachute, humpy, elk hair, wullff, hare's ear, spruce, caddis nymphs, and more. Priced at around $40.

Dave Whitlock's Bass Bug Tying Kit

Approved and designed by Dave Whitlock, the bass bug trying kit provides everything the bass and pike fly-fisherman needs to tie his own bugs and poppers. $60 or so.

Crest 100

Contains a Crest Jr. vise, stainless bobbin, hackle pliers, fly-tying manual, hooks, and an assortment of basic materials for tying popular patterns for Eastern streams. Priced around $40.

Regal Beginner's Fly Kit

This fine beginner's package is one of the most complete kits for the price available. High quality tools, materials, and hooks are provided at a very reasonable price. Around $30.

The Comfortable Fisherman

Most fishermen (and women) would agree that one of the great things about fishing is that there is no dress code. When we go fishing, we can be ourselves, utterly—which means wearing anything from dirty jeans to T-shirts, from plastic mesh baseball caps to jean jackets and sneakers. Of course, some fishermen, and especially fly-fishermen, dress with a little flair and expense in fancy waders and vests, porkpie hats, and astronaut sunglasses. Some Englishmen even wear little rustic tweed suits while fly-fishing, but this is best left to Englishmen, and older ones at that.

However, a fisherman must take his garb seriously whenever and wherever the weather will be cold or rough, or whenever he will be fishing in challenging environments. Anglers should take all wading situations seriously. Water is often cold, fast-moving, and often dangerous. Saltwater wading can take place in precarious situations. Whenever the angler must hike or climb, he must wear proper clothing. Anglers fishing under the hot sun must take certain precautions or risk serious sunburn. In these next pages you should find a few good ideas for making those right sartorial choices—for every fishing situation!

WADING IN

Without waders, a fly-fisherman is just a guy with an expensive stick in his hand. Waders make fly-fishermen "stream-mobile," which is vital. Fly-fishermen must present casts to precise spots on streams and rivers to reach holding or rising trout, and branches and overgrown banks make shore casting on many streams impossible. Surf casting requires waders in colder water, and, of course, waders are essential whenever the boatless freshwater angler needs to cast to a particular spot on the water he can't reach from the shore. Wader styles fall into a neat series of dualities:

Hippers, boots that extend to the waist; and **full-length waders,** boots that extend to the chest for deeper wading.

Felt-soles are better for rocky and pebbly bottoms, and **cleat-soles** better for muddy bottoms.

Boot foot, the standard wader that melds boot and leggings into a single unit, and **slipper foot,** lightweight tight-fitting neoprene or nylon waders that form-fit the body and require wading shoes. The lightness and ease of repair, and packing, make slipper-foot waders the preferred choice of many fly-fishermen.

All waders except the neoprene slipper foot-brand are subject to "weather checking."

THE TACKLE SHOP

BOOT FOOT WADERS

BEST QUALITY

Gra-Lights

This brand offers a heavy-duty, vinyl boot foot with shiny vinyl uppers and cleat soles. A 5-year warranty, repair kit, and suspenders are included. These are among the strongest, sturdiest waders you can buy. About $175.

Orvis Deluxe Stretch Waders

Among the most expensive waders on the market, these super-insulated cadillacs have stretch nylon uppers, anti-chafing, and anti-leak features, and a lining that eliminates clamminess. Priced between $315 to $375.

Ranger Neoprene FS Boot Foot Chest Waders

These neoprene are triple cemented and double taped inside and out to absolutely prevent leaking. Felt soles and built-in front pocket with velcro snaps. Approximately $140 to $180.

Stream-Line Boot Foot Waders $220

Neoprene waders built with Velcro-closed shoulder extension. Felt-soled overshoes are also available. You can't buy a better pair of waders. Priced at around $220.

BEST VALUE

Hodgman Wadewell Waders

These waders are made with 3-ply rubber and are available in cleat or felt soles. Features include front pouch and ozone-deterioration proofing. Excellent value and workmanship for the money. Retail between $65 to $80.

BEST FOR THE BEGINNER

Red Ball Adirondack Waders

Moderately-priced Red Balls that feature fabric-supported uppers, one-piece boot construction with heavy-duty

Waders are essential equipment for fly-fishing.

Courtesy The Orvis Company, Inc.

seams, and cleated outsoles and heels. This lightweight wader is comfortable all day long. Good buy for the occasional angler working in warmer waters and weather. From $40 to $60.

Cabela's Featherlight Boot Foot Waders

These super lightweight nylon boot foot waders with PVC rubber boots are designed with a built-in front pouch and drawstring. About $45.

BOOT FOOT HIPPERS

This is the best wading boot for small streams. In these fly-fishing situations, the angler won't often have to wade much above his thighs. Often the fisherman, standing in water above his waist, is standing in dangerously strong current. Whether you plan to fish on the smaller Eastern chalk streams, Catskills freestone creeks, or moderately-sized rivers, hippers will provide the wading depth you need—with the exception, possibly, of early-spring waters.

Ranger 201 Boot Foot Chest Waders

These waders feature a tough, nylon top coat, and are built like a Chevy truck—tough!—with a raised heel, cushioned insole, and tempered steel shanks. Throw in a 5-year guarantee, and you'll see why this is the best rubber boot Ranger makes. $100 to $145.

Red Ball Master Series Felt-Sole Chest Waders

An excellent combination of durability and comfort in lightweight nylon and rubber construction with heavy-duty seams and one-piece construc-

tion for maximum strength. Built with a nylon drawcord for snug chest fit, reinforced suspender buttons and belt loops, and rustproof hardware. Deep-cleated soles provide plenty of traction in the slippery stuff, and the rubber is treated for ozone resistance. Prices range from $65 to $95.

Orvis Green Mountain Waders

Rugged nylon and rubber construction in fully-vulcanized waders with a cushioned heel and insole. A light, reliable wader. About $100.

BEST QUALITY

Marathon Hip Boots

Marathons are neoprene coated with an insulated wool foot and felt soles. Neoprene means additional warmth and strength: good cold-water boot. Guaranteed for five years, these waders cost about $100.

BEST VALUE

Ranger Lightwade

Lighwades have molded PVC construction and are lined with nylon. They feature reinforced heels, toes, ankles, and shanks with cleat or felt sole. Prices range from $40 to $50.

Hodgman Rod and Reel

The fabric lining in the boot not only provides additional insulation, but comfort, too. These boots make a day on the stream much easier on the feet. About $50.

Red Ball Master Series FS Hip Boot

Built on the wader's specifications, the hipper model is sturdily constructed with 3-ply nylon and rubber layering,

Master Felt-Sole Hip Boot

rustproof hardware, heavy-duty seams, and felt soles. Durable, a little heavier than many models. Priced between $55 and $70.

BEST FOR THE BEGINNER

Red Ball Adirondack FS Hip Boot

Features the same rugged qualities of the wader model (though it is less sturdy than the Master Series): fabric-supported uppers, one-piece construction with heavy-duty seams, and rustproof hardware. These super lightweight boots won't keep you toasty warm in icy winter or in cold, mountain streams, but they are an excellentl choice for the money, priced between $30 and $50 through the mail, or at most fly-fishing shops. A fine hipper for summer wading.

© David Rowley/Envision

Courtesy Cabela's

It's hard to find a good fly-angler who doesn't wear waders. Stocking-foot waders are lighter to wear and easier to repair than boot-foot models.

STOCKING-FOOT WADERS

This is the best technology has to offer in fishing waders. The stocking-foot wader offers so many advantages over traditional rubber waders that it gets hard to be objective! While the stocking-foot wader won't keep you as warm as the rubber boots (which can be alleviated by wearing long johns under your clothes in cold weather), they are lighter, more comfortable, and tighter-fitting. They are also safer when worn with cleat-soled shoes or sneakers, because they give better foot "feel" and control as you work across stream, river, and lake beds. Because the stocking-foot waders are so light, they can be folded into backpacks or knapsacks for back-country hiking or camping, which is impossible with rubber boots.

Stocking-foot prices run a bit higher, and you will probably have to buy a pair of wading shoes—which adds to the expense of course—but many fly-fishermen have assigned boot-foot rubber waders to the ranks of the obselete, and we understand why. But a good pair of stocking-foot waders will last a long time: they are a good investment!

Stocking-foot waders are constructed of either nylon or neoprene, the better insulating and tighter fitting of the two. Neoprene waders are also much easier to repair; any punctures or holes tend to close in on themselves, and are easily sealed with neoprene cement.

THE TACKLE SHOP

BEST QUALITY

Imperial Waders

These neoprene waders are heat-taped, sealed-seam, heavy-duty boots. Imperial makes diving suits and fishing suits for professionals, and knows their way around industrial-strength neoprene. From $140 or so retail.

James-Scott original Boot-Sock Waders

Super-stretchy neoprene construction for freedom of movement and comfort. Built with gravel cuffs, suspenders, quick-release buckles, and draw-string top. Prices fall between $125 and $140. (Add $30-$40 for custom fit.)

Red Ball Premier Neoprene Stocking-Foot Waders

Built with nylon and neoprene layers, these Redballs keep you warm in cold weather and cold water. The "h-back" suspender design comes complete with patch kit and gravel guard. This top wader from a top manufacturer is priced slightly below the competition in the $90 to 100 range.

James-Scott Lined Boot-Sock Waders

Same as above but bonded with nylon-stretch fabric for additional warmth and comfort. About $165.

BEST VALUE

Red Ball Stocking-Foot Hippers and Waders

Made of extremely tough nylon that takes plenty of punishment. This is also a terrific buy at $30 or so for hippers and $40 for waders.

Orvis Lightweight Stocking-Foot Waders and Hippers

Compact, lightweight waders and hippers (the waders weigh only 12 ozs.), these nylon models are tightly sealed and guaranteed not to leak or pull apart. Light enough to pack away for hiking to a favorite stream or lake. From $35 for hippers and $45 for waders.

BEST FOR THE BEGINNER

Ranger Lightweight Stocking-Foot Waders and Hippers

Tough and durable, 2-ply nylon construction for small stream wading. Great buy for the cost-conscious angler at around $25 to $28.

Red Ball Sportster Waders

Made with nylon, these Red Balls come in all sizes and are priced from about $18 to $25.

Red Ball Master Flyweight ST Hip Boots

Courtesy Red Ball, Inc.

WADING SHOES

Those of you choosing stocking-foot waders will need to wear high traction shoes over the waders. Many fishermen use sneakers, and a good pair will do well on softer-bottom streams—mud, silt, and pebbles. However, in faster currents, on rockier bottoms, and on any stream or river bed with treacherous footing, wading shoes are the safer choice.

BEST QUALITY

Hodgman Lakestream Neoprene Stocking-Foot Waders

Ideal for colder waters and float tubing, this heavy-duty, sponge-cushioned wader offers maximum comfort in cold and wet conditions. With 3-ply reinforced-neoprene sponge construction, the angler is well-insulated against cold and abrasions. Adjustable and removable suspenders allow conversion to waist high wear. Front pocket with Velcro zipper and permanent gravel cuffs. Excellent wader for larger, colder, Western and Alaskan waters. Top quality. $100 is the price range.

Orvis Lightweight Wading Shoe

These shoes feature man-made leather uppers, reinforced toes, and felt or cleated soles. About $60 to 70.

Gary Borger's Ultimate Wading Shoe

Leather uppers (man-made); triple-thickness felt soles, padded collar, hard plastic toe. From $50 to $80.

Red Ball Flyweight S/T Chest Waders

Lightweight Orvis Wading Shoes

BEST VALUE

Red Ball Master Wading Shoe

Made with nylon uppers, felt soles, and vents, these shoes are about $40.

BEST FOR THE BEGINNER

River Systems Out West

Velcro lacing, brown nylon uppers with yellow toes; steel shank, felt or cleated soles, padded ankle tops. About $40.

VESTED INTERESTS

It would be harder to find a fly-fisherman without a fly vest, than to find an artist without a set of paints.

Carrying an array of flies, leaders, extra lines, extra clippers, and extra reels offers the fly-fishing angler a degree of security: he can be confident that he won't be caught short no matter the situation. Without the vest, holding even the minimum equipment necessary to effectively fish on a familiar stream—one fly box, extra terminal leader material, fly floatant, extra sunglasses, a clipper, and forceps—means that your pants pockets will be pretty full, and pants pockets are difficult to reach when wading in water over your waist. So even the modestly ambitious fly-fisherman should treat himself to a fly-fishing vest, albeit a simple one.

The most important matter to consider in buying a fly vest is the number of pockets. Only the most seasoned fly-fisherman angling in the most challenging and unknown

conditions really needs a thirty-five-pocket fly vest such as the Orvis Super Tac L Pac. Most fly-fishermen would have a hard time filling up eighteen pockets. The intermediate fly-fisherman probably only needs fifteen- to twenty-pockets—beginners no more than ten pockets.

You'll be wearing your loaded vest all day, so remember that it should be comfortable around your neck and back. Many vest designers are now stitching an elastic neck band atop the vest, which helps distribute the weight more comfortably. Don't forget that bright-colored clothing might scare trout, so buy a neutral colored vest brown, tan, dark green, or gray. Always carefully examine the prospective vest for the details of quality worksmanship—secure velcro, zippers, or stitching. When you find the right vest, load it up, and hang it on a nail, ready for the first hatch of spring on your favorite sweetheart-of-a-trout stream.

The fly-fishing vest should provide enough pockets to carry floatant, flies, leaders, extra line, clippers, sunglasses, fly line, and forceps.

T H E   T A C K L E   S H O P

BEST QUALITY

Patagonia Fishing Vest

This super lightweight 10.5 ounce wading vest is made with cool, water-repellent rip-stop nylon, and nylon mesh. Short and cool for deep-water, hot-weather wading, this is a great vest for the flats fisherman. Around $75 at most retail tackle stores.

Fothergill Designs Vest

The Fothergill has fifteen pockets with a nylon-knit collar for load bearing comfort, a self-contained carry bag, tote straps on back for coat, rod, and thermos. About $85 to $95.

Orvis Super Tac-L Pac

Orvis' best vest comes with thirty-five pockets, both inside and out. Special features in-clude two pockets on the back for reels and extra spools, and maximum-security zippered pockets for small items like pockets knives and keys. A support yoke across the back distributes the weight, and the knit collar prevents chafing. Plenty of velcro and zippers the whole way around to keep everything safe. Priced at about $65.

Stream Designs the Classic

This twenty-five-pocket vest includes a forceps holster, rod holder, back pouch, and zippered back pocket. About $75.

Columbia Sportswear Deschutes

Great vest for the money, with thirteen pockets. Prices start at around $40.

Simms Master Vest

Knit collar, Velcro pockets, rustproof zippers, and other top-quality features found in most high-priced vests. Made of nylon mesh with sixteen pockets. $80 and up.

BEST VALUE

Columbia Henry's Fork II

This vest features an additional zippered flap placed over three inside tippet-spool pockets for more storage area. Neck is lined with a special yoke, and all thirteen front pockets are double stitched with Velcro closures. Offers 2D rings, double-back pockets for reels, and comes in a variety of dark colors: a first-rank vest for less money than other top-of-the-line makes. $50 or so at most outlets.

Scoopmouth

© M. Timothy O'Keefe/Tom Stack & Associates

Orvis Super Tac-L Pac

© Greg L. Ryan

This fly fisherman just landed a rainbow trout in an Eastern Wisconsin river.

BEST FOR THE BEGINNERS

Orvis Simplicity Vest

Terrific quality but the six pockets may not be enough for all fishermen, though it is probably enough for many. Back pouch has snap closure, the two large front pockets are zippered. $19.50.

Thomas & Thomas Adult Value Vest

Seven pockets, two t-rings for keys, forceps, and clippers. Priced at about $20.

LL Bean Shorty

This comfortable, lightweight short vest is made from 100-percent ripstop cotton for cool fishing even on the hottest days. Nine large outside pockets, and five inside pockets provide all the storage capacity most fly-fishermen will need. Prices start at about $50.

Thomas & Thomas

Orvis Simplicity Vest

FOUL WEATHER FRIENDS

It often seems that the more fishing one does, the more bad weather one encounters. Without question, serious fishermen eventually confront serious weather (just ask the steelhead angler!). Failure to wear proper clothing can mean the difference, not only between pleasure and misery, but between sickness and health. So be ready for the cold, the wet, the humid, and the hot.

Bad weather and good fly-fishing often go together.

THE TACKLE SHOP

WADING AND RAIN JACKETS

Barbour Gamefair Jacket

The Prince of Wales wears Barbour jackets—that's how good they are. Each jacket is made of the finest Egyptian cotton, oiled and waxed to provide maximum weatherproofing with a minimum of condensation. The Gamefair jacket features a corduroy collar in brown, studs for hoods, press-studded throat flap, stormfly front, raglan sleeves with underarm ventilation, adjustable storm cuffs, brass finish, two-way metal zipper, two large bellows pockets with storm flaps, pure-cotton tartan lining, and studs for optional warm pile lining. By Jove, now that's a jacket! From $175.

Patagonia Rain Jacket

Patogonia's new sawed-off rain jacket, made of lightweight nylon ripstop, coated with Seal Coat and bonded to a fine, tricot scrim, might be perfect for the fly-fishermen who plans to fish where the weather can take a nasty turn. The sleeves allow easy casting motion, are water repellant, and the full-length two-way front zipper, as well as the slanted side pockets, are protected by double storm flaps. The hood has a reinforced visor. Priced from around $100 to $150.

Gortex Wading Parka

A short wading jacket that offers large Velcro-closed front pockets, elastic waist with fully gusseted, Velcro-adjustable cuffs. About $120.

Kool Dri Wading Jacket

Waterproof, breathable, light, and tough rainwear with adjustable drawstring at the bottom. Two breast pockets, elastic cuffed sleeves, and adjustable hood. From $55. Good deal.

GLOVES

Glacier Gloves

Extremely warm gloves made of closed-cell neoprene. Thumb and finger tips are made with nylon for additional feel, and the index and thumb covers are slit so fishermen can do detail work without removing the gloves—or finger covers. Around $40 or so.

Orvis Nonabsorbing Fishing Gloves

Warm nonabsorbing polyester can be wrung out when wet and will dry instantly. Nylon-knit cuffs keep wrists protected from cold, wind, and briars. About $8.

DuPont Sports Guard Gloves

Made of Kevlar, a super-tough material used in bulletproof vests, these gloves protect the hands whether you're filleting

Mellar Mitts

a fish, handling a toothy pike or bluefish, gutting a deer, or working around the yard. Hundreds of tiny rubber palm buttons make your grip secure. You can catch a bullet with these babies.

Patagonia Fingerless Fishing Gloves

Bunting fabric, rib-knit cuffs. $17 or so.

SUNGLASSES

Orvis Battenkill Polarized Sunglasses

Scratch-resistant, polarized lenses, aviator-style frames. $28.

Orvis Fishing Hat

Foster Grant Sportglasses

Polarized lenses with wrap-around fit for extra eye protection. Spring-tension temples hold glasses firmly in place. $12 or so.

Ray Ban Outdoorsman Glasses

These aviator-style shades with polarized lenses offer crystal-sharp, no-glare vision. Extra-large lenses are precision optical quality, and shaded neutral-gray for accurate color translation. From $40 at local outdoors or tackle shops, or through the mail. These are the best.

Orvis Battenkill Polarized Sunglasses

Roland Martin Pro View Fishing Glasses

Aluminum frame, and "patented amber colored Tri-X polarized glass" with side-shade protectors to dispel glare. About $12.

HATS

Orvis Fishing Hat

Offers shade for the eyes and the back of the neck. Made with water-repellent poplin. About $120.

Flats Stalker

Visor and attachable neck cover provide complete sun protection. $10.

THERMAL UNDERWEAR

Blue Johns

100-percent chlorofibre with three times the insulating capacity of cotton, and nearly twice that of wool and polypropylene. Lowest moisture absorption of any fiber, keeping wetness away from the body to keep you dry. Non-allergenic, and non-flammable. $30 to $35, depending on retail outlet or catalog.

Orvis Silk Underwear

Light, warm, moisture-absorbing silk that beats cotton and many other fibers in warmth and dryness...and feels soooo good. $20.

Holly Hansen Long Johns

These "Montana tested" longies are made with an inner layer of polypropylene that allows the body's moisture to pass directly to the outer layer of absorbent wool. $25.

Courtesy The Orvis Company, Inc.

Orvis Silk Underwear

FINISHING TOUCHES

A solid, sturdy tackle box, a fine landing net, a rod case for travel: these are some of the important extras an angler can reward himself with after a few fishing expeditions that provide the full flavor, both sweet and sour, of America's greatest sport. Do you love it? Then complete your outfit.

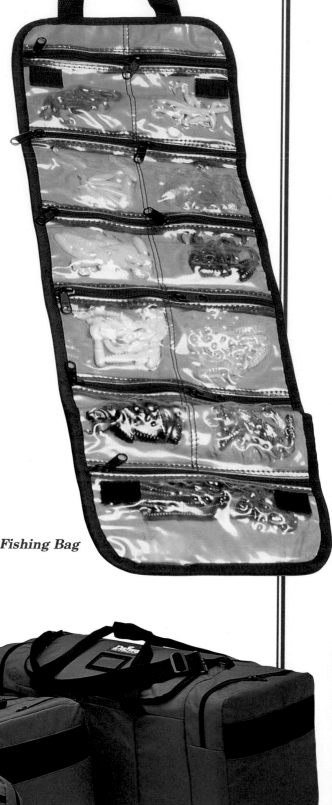

Cabela's Tackle Satchel

Cabela's Fishing Bag

Daiwa satchels

THE TACKLE SHOP

TACKLE BOXES

Flambeau Adventurer Boxes

Large tackle boxes in a variety of sizes for the freshwater and saltwater angler. Models are equipped with as many as five drawers and fifty-three compartments, or as small as three drawers with thirty-two compartments, or, for the beginning angler, a two tray, twenty-five compartment box, which costs around $15, with prices on larger models up to $85.

Plano Tackle Boxes

Plano makes many different styles of large and small plastic freshwater and saltwater tackle boxes, though Plano specializes in chests for the bass and crappie fisherman. Special models are designed for spinner baits, crappie fishing, pork rinds, and for complex bass fishing that includes large boxes such as the Plano 787 which holds four spinnerbait racks, four wormproof drawers, and extra bottom drawer, all held together with two strong latches on top and one below. From $14 or $15 at the smallest, ranging up to $40 for a very large one.

Trophy Tackle Boxes

Largely designed for saltwater fishing, the Trophy box is made of crushproof polypropylene and is fitted with a recessed drop handle. Features cantilever action wormproof trays and double-cam action safety latches. Stainless steel hinges and pins. Three models, with three trays and eight compartments for large lures and rigs. Priced from $12 to $30.

ROD CASES

Orvis Aluminum Rod Case

Heavy-walled aluminum tubing, machined screw cap. In various sizes—$20 to $30.

Fenwick Hi-Tech 67 Rod and Reel Satchel

Transports and protects rigged, ready to fish rods. Capacity for eight rods. Includes four steel-reinforced fail-proof latches, with tight-fitting tongue and groove flanges to keep out rain and spray. About $40.

Plano Rod Case

4¼-inch-diameter rod case has unique hinged door at top, which can be opened for loading. Collapse-proof locking collar is adjustable for various sized rods. $30 or so.

James Scott Rod Case

Built of nylon cordura over PVC tubing, this case holds up to four rods in their cloth bags, or two rods in aluminum tubes. Lockable zipper, carrying handle, adjustable shoulder bag. $40 or so.

DB Dun Rod Case

Among the finest rod cases on the market, the DB Dun is crafted from the best materials, including high-quality denier-nylon Cordura and strong aluminum tubing. These cases include a baffle within each tube that makes each rod section its own compartment. In 50", 57", 60", and 65" lengths, and a variety of tube diameters. Priced from $35 to $60.

Courtesy The Orvis Company, Inc.

Orvis Aluminum Rod Cases

ENDGAME

After winning the battle against your piscine quarry, you will either return him to his watery home, or, well, you know what to do if you like seafood. Nets and gaffes make it much easier to manage the landed fish and do with him as you will.

Orvis Madison Nets

Beautiful, bamboo-mahogany-ash laminate. Soft-dacron net bag that won't hurt release-able fish. $35 or so.

Cascade Lakes Teardrop Landing Nets

Narrow-bowed nets for back-packing in the backcountry. 2-ply ash bows. Tapered, brown cotton net bag. Largely for trout. In sizes from 18" to 24", and prices from $28.

Pepper Nets

These wood landing nets of ma-hogany and ash come with a large tapered cotton net bag.
Aluminum nets are light-weight and durable with a built-in retract-able net cord.
Wood Net 19", 20", 21". About $20-$25.
Aluminum Net 18" or 19" $7 to $10.

Excaliber Weight Scale Net

Catch fish and settle bets at the same time. You'll phone in those world-records right away with this special net. Handle has a built-in weight scale that measures between 0 and 20 pounds. $20.

Aftco Flying Gaff

Shafts are 6 feet long and hooks are anodized with a gold finish, and fitted with two black, non-slip grips. "Flying" means hook detaches from handle. About $30.

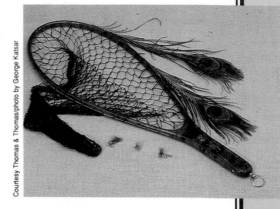

Courtesy Thomas & Thomas/photo by George Katsar

T&T Heritage Walnut Net

Pompanette Gaffs

Anodized-aluminum handles and stainless steel hooks . . . OUCH! Floats if dropped over-board. $20-$40 in sizes from 2-feet to 8-feet handles, and 2-inch to 4-inch hooks.

Aftco Tapered Aluminum Gaffs

Sizes from 4-feet to 8-feet han-dles and 2-inch to 3-inch hooks.

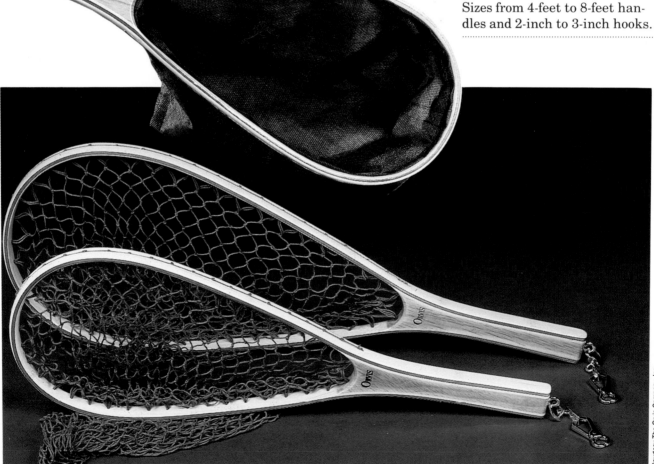

Orvis Nets

Courtesy The Orvis Company, Inc.

© Barry & Cathy Beck Photo

© Barry & Cathy Beck Photo

Nets are essential for catch-and-release fly fishing, allowing the angler to release the fish without overhandling. Nets are also handy for making sure "keepers" go in the creel.

© Hanson Carroll/FPG International

APPENDIX

The Angler's Database

BOOKS

THE FRESHWATER SHELF

Art Flick's Streamside Guide to Naturals and Their Imitations
by Art Flick
Nick Lyons Books

The benchmark work on identifying the little buggies and creepy-crawlers trout eat, and how to match them with the flies in your vest. Essential for the beginning fly-fisherman.

Trout
by Ray Bergman
Knopf

First published in 1938, by Knopf, and still in print with a new 1984 edition, this remains an all-time favorite: "The only true American angling classic still widely read is Ray Bergman's *Trout.... Trout* remains our Old Testament, the first and only book many anglers look to for guidance."— Harmon Henkin, *The New York Times*.

North America's Freshwater Fishing Book
by Mike Rosenthal
Scribner

A comprehensive guide to catching twenty-two of the most popular gamefish in the United States and Canada. Rosenthal offers plenty of fishing tips, but the distinguishing mark of this book is his warm, self-deprecating prose. Touched with his awareness of the mysteries of fish and fishing, which fascinate all of us, but are so hard to catch in language. You'll learn how to catch carp, suckers, catties, trout, and bass.

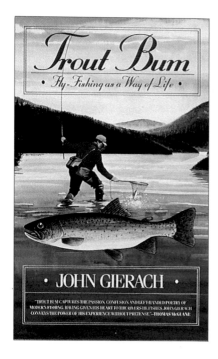

Trout Bum
by John Gierach
Fireside Books/Simon & Schuster

This collection of essays on the pleasures, satisfactions, and bitter ironies of life as a "trout bum," by the cranky, but endearing, John Gierach, earned—and deserves—high praise. "Captures the passion, confusion, and left-handed poetry of modern fishing better than any other book...."
—Thomas McGuane

The Well-Tempered Angler
by Arnold Gingrich
Plume

Now in paperback, this book collects the angling wisdom and reminiscences of the late *Esquire* magazine chief who hung out with every legend of the Beaverkill.

Fishless Days, Angling Nights
by Sparse Grey Hackle
Fireside Books/Simon & Schuster

The collected pieces of the late Alfred W. Miller, the "poet laureate of American trout fishing"—*Field and Stream*. Humorous, evocative, full of myths, tall tales, and idiosyncratic histories of a peculiar American sub-culture.

In the Ring of the Rise
by Vince Marinaro
Nick Lyons Books

The late, crotchety genius from Carlisle, Pennsylvania, cataloged the varieties of trout feeding and rising behavior in a classic work.

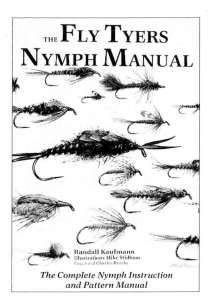

Fly Tyer's Nymph Manual
by Randall Kaufmann
Western Fisherman's Press

"This book is definitely a winner," says Gary LaFontaine of *Field & Stream*. Everything the budding and intermediate tier of nymph flies should know is found right here. And nymphs are the perfect patterns for beginners to try, because they are easier to tie than dry and wet flies.

Tactics on Trout
by Ray Ovington
Scribner

Advice on casting for trout and hooking trout, in thirty-three different trout-fishing situations, by the author of over forty books on fishing and the outdoors.

The Book of Fly Patterns
by Eric Leiser
Knopf

Master-tier Eric Leiser has written the most complete book on modern fly patterns available—with tying instructions for many new and unusual patterns. This beautifully designed book is packed with razor-sharp photos.

The Flytier's Almanac
edited by Robert H. Boyle and Dave Whitlock
Nick Lyons Books

An excellent middle-level reference work for the flytier, with lots of new information for the growing tier.

A River Runs Through It
by Norman Maclean
University of Chicago Press

A father and his two sons, fly-fishing, and what some would call the meaning of life. Really. One of the finest fishing books written by an American author in our time.

Bright Rivers
by Nick Lyons
Fireside Books/Simon & Schuster

A "moving, perceptive, beautifully written" (*The New York Times*) account of a city-dweller's love affair with wild rivers and trout. Irresistible reading by the author of "The Seasonable Angler" column in *Fly Fisherman*.

The Atlantic Salmon
by Lee Wulff
Nick Lyons Books

While never a bestseller, *The Atlantic Salmon* remains as the only book to buy about catching Atlantic salmon, which for many fly-fishermen, and other anglers, is the premiere gamefish in the world. Wulff has caught them everywhere, from Nova Scotia to Iceland to Sweden.

The Even-Tempered Angler
by Louis D. Rubin, Jr.
Winchester Press

The humorous accounts of a North Carolina University professor's bottom-fishing exploits, and his scalpel-sharp parodies of other fishermen, in this light masterpiece modeled on Izaak Walton's famous book, *The Compleat Angler.*

Caddisflies
by Gary LaFontaine
Nick Lyons Books

Everything you need to know about one of the trout's favorite meals.

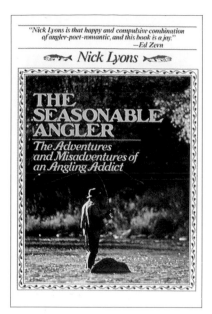

"Nick Lyons is that happy and compulsive combination of angler-poet-romantic, and this book is a joy."
—Ed Zern

Nick Lyons

THE SEASONABLE ANGLER
The Adventures and Misadventures of an Angling Addict

The Seasonable Angler
by Nick Lyons
Fireside Books/Simon & Schuster

His first book, chronicling, with self-deprecating wit, the personal history of a dedicated fly-fisherman.

American Fly Fishing: A History
by Paul Schullery
Nick Lyons Books

One of America's best natural history and fishing authors looks at the 250-year history of fly-fishing. He explores its values, rivers, traditions, technologies, and great innovators.

The Complete Book of Fly-Tying
by Eric Leiser
Knopf/Random House

Leiser's complete introduction to fly-tying is written with eloquent clarity, empathy for the beginner, a sense of the importance of fly-tying to the sport, and illustrations at all the right places including detailed line drawings that make each step easy to follow. The best book for the learning flytier.

Nymphs
by Ernest Schweibert
Winchester Press

The classic study of the immature stages of the aquatic fly hatches, which amount to 90 percent of the trout's normal diet. The text is brilliantly complimented by Schweibert's amazingly detailed color paintings, which give practical, visual help for identification.

Bass Wars
by Nick Taylor
McGraw-Hill

Life in the peculiar American culture of bass tournaments and Southern bass-master celebrities. Outstanding personal journalism.

Trout Madness and Trout Magic
by Robert Traver
Fireside Books/Simon & Schuster

Two very popular collections. Traver offers a different kind of fishing writing: acerbic, sharp, full of the joys and wonder of catching trout in the beautiful Michigan upcountry, but clear-eyed about the prices of our pleasures.

Bass Fishing Fundamentals
by Ken Schultz
Stephen Green Press/Viking

"An excellent, practical book for both the beginner and the expert."—Nelson Bryant, *The New York Times.*

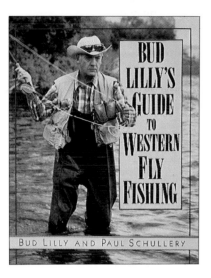

Bud Lilly's Guide to Western Fly-Fishing
by Bud Lilly and
Paul Schullery
Nick Lyons Books

The most complete and reliable guide to hooking the big trout and steelies of the West and Northwest by one of the great trout fisherman around. Don't fly-fish the West without reading this book.

Selective Trout
by Doug Swisher and
Carl Richards
Winchester Press

One of the most important fly-fishing books ever published, this took the biggest step ever in fly-fishing methodology because it explains why trout prefer certain flies over others at different times. Not for the blush-cheeked initiate. This is technical. And its advice requires hours of field work on the water to apply successfully.

THE SALTWATER SHELF

Modern Saltwater Fishing
by Vic Dunaway
Winchester Press

Solid instruction from a highly-informed expert on fishing the briny.

Blues
by John Hersey
Vintage/Random House

A dialogue between the Fisherman and the Stranger, about blues, and fishing for them, and what they can teach us about nature. "*Blues* informs and enlightens in the grand tradition of open-air, universe-in-a-grain-of-sand writing.... Part philosophy, part natural history, part cookbook, part fishing lore, this is a book as singular as its author...." —*The Baltimore Sun.*

Fly-Fishing in Saltwater
by Lefty Kreh
Nick Lyons Books

A complete guide to going after redfish, permit, tarpon, and bonefish on the saltwater flats and elsewhere.

Bluefishing
by Henry Lyman
Nick Lyons Books

The former publisher of *Saltwater Sportsman* has written the complete book about catching bluefish—where to stalk them, lures, tackle, baits, techniques, and a special fly-rodding section.

Striped Bass Fishing
by Frank Woolner and
Hal Lyman
Nick Lyons Books

The complete guide to catching stripers, covering tackle, artificial and live baitfishing, jettie, dock, boat, and surf techniques, with attention to catching these hot fish on fly tackle.

THE REFERENCE SHELF

The Simon & Schuster Pocket Guide to Trout and Salmon Flies
by John Buckland
Fireside Books/Simon & Schuster

A field book for fly identification in stores and on the water.

McClane's New Standard Fishing Encyclopedia
by A. J. McClane
Holt, Rhinehart

The ultimate guide to everything about fishing and fish—tackle, technique, species, regions, methods, and recipes.

Orvis Index of Fly Patterns
Orvis

A comprehensive guide to 355 Orvis fly patterns for trout, salmon, tarpon, bonefish, and permit.

Trout Vols. I & II.
by Ernest Schweibert
Dutton

Back in print, the overwhelming masterpiece on trout biology, trout angling, and trout everything.

Hook, Line, and Sinker: The Complete Angler's Guide to Terminal Tackle
by Gary Soucie
Fireside Books/Simon & Schuster

Everything you need to know about hooks, sinkers, snaps, swivels, floats, lines, leaders, lures, and knots to catch more fish in freshwater or saltwater. Tackle and techniques that will spell the difference between a trophy catch and "the one that got away." "The reference manual to put all others to shame."—*Field & Stream.*

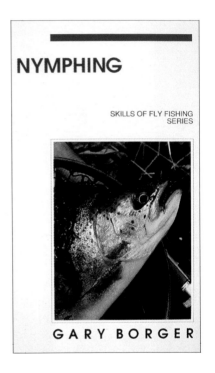

VIDEOS

GARY BORGER VIDEOS: "These are all exceptional videos of the genre.... [T]his guy is a serious contender for top-gun in a crowded field."—*Rod & Reel.*

"...sets a standard of excellence for the instructional use of film in teaching hard-to-learn fly-fishing techniques."—John Randolph, in *Fly Fisherman.*

Nymphing
30 minutes

The original, instructional fly-fishing film, shot on Montana's spectacular Armstrong Spring Creek where nymph-fishing is truly superb. Trout, especially the big ones, feed under the surface ninety percent of the time. This tape shows you all the nymph-fishing tactics.

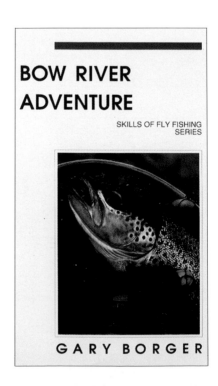

South Island Sampler
60 minutes

Gary Borger takes the viewer on an action-filled expedition to the South Island of New Zealand, where he travels with friends to exotic wilderness areas by helicopter, jet boat, light aircraft, Land Rover, and foot. There they stalk the great 20-inch rainbow and brown trout. Lots of great photography and action-filled shots, as well as lessons on all the key techniques for spotting and casting to nervous, lunker New Zealand trout.

Bow River Adventure
60 minutes

Borger leads the viewer to world-class dry-fly fishing for huge trout on Canada's incredible Bow River. Month-long insect hatches of unbelievable intensity bring the big rainbows and browns to the surface where Borger and other fly-fishermen can take 'em. Plenty of clear information and great camera work explain the hatches, the insects, how to match them, and the best tackle for taking large, wild trout on the Bow.

TROUT IN STILLWATERS

SKILLS OF FLY FISHING SERIES

GARY BORGER

The Fabulous Bighorn
60 minutes

With over 6,000 fish per mile, the Bighorn River is one of the United States' premier trout streams. More great camera work and terrific advice on fishing with nymphs and dry flies for big rainbows and browns.

Trout in Stillwaters
60 minutes

Techniques for taking trout on lakes around the world. The best places to find trout, how to spot cruisers, the principle food organisms of lakes, and how these organisms' life cycles fit into a trout's food web.

JACK DENNIS FLY TYING SERIES
One of the best tiers of Western fly patterns explains numerous tying secrets, as well as providing interesting fly-fishing advice, and some great action photography.

Tying Western Trout Flies
120 minutes.

Detailed, step-by-step explanations. Learn to tie Humpys, Wulffs, the Elk Hair Caddis, and Muddler Minnows.

Tying Western Dry Flies
120 minutes.

Features Mike Lawson tying No Hackles, Floating Nymphs, and other favorites. Plenty of action shots.

Tying and Fishing the Caddisfly
120 minutes.

Gary LaFontaine and Mike Lawson fish with the caddisfly on the Snake, Henry's Fork, and Yellowstone Rivers. Fly-tying tips with Jack Dennis.

Fly-Tying Basics
60 minutes.

Jack Dennis explains the fundamentals.

Angler's Guide to New Zealand
60 minutes.

Jack Dennis takes the viewer into the Rangitaki and Tongariro Rivers of the Lake Taupo area for spectacular rainbow and brown trout fishing.

LEFTY KREH FLY FISHING SERIES
One of the world's best-known fly-fishermen covers a number of important fly-fishing subjects in reasonable depth, and provides one great mouthwatering action sequence after another.

Lefty Kreh's Exciting World of Saltwater Fly-Fishing
45 minutes

Join Lefty on the flats of Belize and learn fly casting and fishing techniques for bonefish, barracuda, and tarpon.

Fly-Fishing the Bow River with Lefty Kreh
30 minutes.

Fly-fishing various waters with various techniques on the great Bow River.

Light Tackle Tips with Lefty Kreh
30 minutes.

How to save time, money, and energy, fishing with light tackle.

Fly Casting Techniques with Lefty Kreh
30 minutes.

Step-by-step.

Fly-fishing for Bass with Dave Whitlock
60 minutes.

America's premier bass-poppin' and fly-fishin' expert leads the viewer through every essential area of knowledge, from equipment to flies to technique, and why the big hogs do what they do. Plenty of beautiful, compelling underwater footage. A real gem of a tape. Get it.

Bass Mastery Series with Al Lindner Vols. I, II, & III

Top-production quality and exciting bass-catchin' footage by leading tackle (and everything else!) manufacturer, 3M, with the advice and direction of Bass Master Al Lindner.

I: Catching Bass in Natural Lakes: The Basic Principles
60 minutes.

Where to find bass as seasons change, how bass relate to their environment, and how to use this information to pick the right lure, and other equipment.

II: Catching Bass in Natural Lakes: Spring Period
60 minutes.

How bass relate to emerging cover in a lake. Best lures and strategies for catching active, roaming bass.

III: Catching Bass in Natural Lakes: Summer Period
60 minutes.

Understanding the diversity of bass movement and location during the summer, the most complex angling time of the year, means you will need to know how to pick the right lure, and know how to use it, and where to use it. This tape shows you how.

IV: Catching Bass in Natural Lakes: Fall Period
60 minutes.

The fall is when trophy fish are most likely to be caught. Handling the transition from warm water to cool, and finding and catching bass in deeper waters.

BABE WINKLEMAN VIDEOS

The following tapes are only a fraction of the enormous number of videos the prolific Babe Winkleman has produced over the past few years. This guy cuts a lot of good bass videos, and the following are particularly good.

Largemouth Bass I

Techniques in various kinds of cover. Casting, lure selection, and more.

Largemouth Bass II

Breakthrough techniques including Bass and Rice, and frog-run bassin', and busting bass off the flats.

Smallmouth Bass I

Exciting breakthrough techniques for taking smalls. Early spring to late fall.

Smallmouth Bass II

Where to find them, proper lure selection, seasonal movements.

Fly-Fishing Video Magazine

This is a smart business venture, indeed. Subscribers to Fly-Fishing Video Magazine receive six video tapes a year for an annual subscription rate of what is now $150. Individual tapes are priced at $50. Although these tapes are expensive, they provide a combination of great landscape and fishing drama, mixed with basic tips on improving techniques for each kind of fly-fishing, and worth the price. Nelson Bryant of the *New York Times* called the photography "outstanding." Videos in the series have, so far, visited Be-lize, for tarpon and bonefish fly-fishing on the flats; the Skagit and Sauk rivers in Washington for steelheads; caught the magic of salmon, trout, and grayling fishing on the Alagnak River in Alaska; returned to Washington for rainbow trout fishing; visited the Ayakulik River in Alaska for King salmon; and followed a spring float down the Missouri and Yellowstone rivers for more trout fishing. For more information, contact:

Fly-Fishing Video Magazine
4f853 152nd Place S.E.
Bellevue, Washington 98006
(800) 327-2893

FISHING OUTFITTERS

Adventure. If you want the real thing, and are ready to pay for it: huge legendary gamefish, exotic settings and men and women with stories to keep you up half the night drinking by the fire. Fish you only thought existed in fishing magazines. Contact one of these companies for an unforgettable adventure.

Adventure Safaris Ltd.
3 First National Plaza
Suite 747
Chicago, IL 60602

Angler Adventures
Crossroads Travel
Route 2
Lyme, CT 06371
New Zealand and Alaska

Angler's Travel
c/o Eddie Bauer
220 Post Street
San Francisco, CA 94108

© Paul Zimmerman

New Zealand Trout Fishing
Tongariro Lodge/North Island
 Host & Guide: Tony Hayes
Rotoroa Lodge/South Island
 Host & Guide: Bob Haswell
Cedar Lodge/South Island Host
 & Guide: Tony Hayes
All types of fly-fishing for
 trophy rainbows and browns.
Iceland:
Laxa i Adaldal
Thorskafjordura

Frontiers International
P.O. Box 161
Wexford, PA

Alagnak Lodge
4117 Hillcrest Way P.O. 7
Sacramento, CA 95821
Alaska salmon and steelhead.

Beartooth Plateau Outfitters
P.O. Box 1127
Cooke City, MT 59020
Yellowstone/Alaska-Beartooth
 National Wilderness Area
 fishing trips.

Bressler Outfitters, Inc.
Star Route 45-B
Jackson Hole, WY 83001
South Fork, Teton, New Fork,
 Green, and Snake Rivers.

Club Pacific
790 27th Avenue
San Francisco, CA 94121
Mel Kreiger: Argentina, New
 Zealand, Alaska, France,
 Mexico, Bahamas, Australia.

Fishing International
4000 Montgomery Dr.
Santa Rosa, CA 95405
Lani Waller: Alaska,
 Caribbean, Central America,
 New Zealand, Christmas
 Island, South America.

The Flyfisher
315 Columbine St.
Denver, CO 80206
 Colorado trout fishing.

Gates AuSable Lodge
Rt. 2
Grayling, MI 49738
Wade the famous AuSable
 River for wild trout.

Kaufmanns Fly-Fishing
 Expeditions, Inc.
P.O. Box 23032
Portland, OR 97223
New Zealand, Alaska,
 Argentina, France, Austria,
 Christmas Island, Bahamas,
 Baja, Yucatan, Costa Rica.

Ken Tours
5825 Kanan Road
Agoura, CA 91301
New Zealand.

Outdoor Safaris
P.O. Box 6366
Hollywood, FL 33021
New Zealand, Alaska,
 Argentina.

Pan Angling Travel Service
180 N. Michigan Ave.
Chicago, IL 60601

Paul Roos Outfitters
1630 Leslie
Helena, MT 59601
Montana blue-ribbon trout

Sportsmen's Travel Service
119 E. Palatine Road
Palatine, IL 60067
Alaska, Canada

Thomas & Thomas
Fly-Fishing Adventures
P.O. Box 32, 22 Third Street
Turners Falls, MA 01376
Canada, Scandinavia, South
 America, Alaska, Central
 America

Wilderness Water Ways
625 N.W. Starker Ave.
Corvallis, OR 97330
Fish the Deschutes, Rogue,
 and Umpqua Rivers for
 rainbows, steelhead, and
 bass.

Worldwide Sportsman
P.O. Drawer 787
Islamorada, FL 33036
Caribbean, Central America

FLY FISHING SCHOOLS

Yes, yes, we know we said it
was easy, but it ain't easy till
you know *how*. These schools
will provide all the important
background you'll need on
casting technique and fly selection and presentation, which in
essence means that you won't
have to read as many fly-
fishing books, and you'll get to
learn with other people, which
is fun. However, most of the
learn-to-fly fish programs are
fairly expensive, running to
the hundreds of dollars for a
weekend of instruction. Books
are cheaper, but you'll still
have to practice anyway.
 Before you join a school, try
a little fly-fishing on your own
to be sure of your interest.
Fishing money is a terrible
thing to waste.

FLY FISHING SCHOOLS
L.L. Bean Fly-Fishing School
Freeport, ME 04033
Dave Whitlock

Beckie's Fly-Fishing
 Specialists
1336 Orange St.
Berwick, PA 18603
Cathy and Barry Beck

Big Hole River Outfitters
P.O. Box 366
Dillon, MT 59725
Chuck Fothergill

Brightwaters Fly-Fishing
 School
3803 Grand Avenue South
Minneapolis, MN 55409
Tom Hegelson

Creative Sports Enterprises
2333 Boulevard Circle
Walnut Creek, CA 94595

© Billy E. Barnes/FPG International

K Bar L Fly-Fishing School
1272 Highland Drive
Moscow, ID 83843
Dave Engerbretson

FENWICK FLY SCHOOLS
East:
7003 Glen Court
Frederick, MD 21701
Jim Gilford

Midwest:
309 South 11th Ave
Wausau, WN 54401
Gary Borger

West:
790 27th Avenue
San Francisco, CA 94121
Mel Kreiger

Montana:
Marketing Department,
 Fenwick
P.O. Box 729
Westminster, CA 92684
Bob Kelly

Vince Cummings Fly-Fishing
 Clinics
RD 1
Box 124A
Roscoe, NY 12776
Jim Peterson

Eddie Bauer, Inc.
21110 Greenfield Road
Oak Park, MI 48237
Chuck MacDonald

Frustrated Fisherman's Fly
 School
950 Highway 93 South
Victor, MT 59875
Doug Swisher

Hunter's Angling Supplies
Central Square Box 300
New Boston, NH 03070
Lefty Kreh and Richard
 Talleur

Kaufmann's Fly Fishing
 School
Kaufmann's Streamborn Flies
P.O. Box 23032
Portland, OR 97223
Learn on the Deschutes River!

Montana School of Fly Fishing
Box 6
Nye, MT 59061

Orvis Fly Fishing Schools
10 River Road
Manchester, VT 05254

Orvis West Coast Fly Fishing
   Schools
166 Maiden Lane
San Francisco, CA 94108
Brant Oswald

Powell Rod Co.
P.O. Box 3966
Chico, CA 95927
Pres Powell

Thomas & Thomas Fly Fishing
   Schools
P.O. Box 32
Turners Falls, MA 01376

Joan and Lee Wulff Fishing
   School
Beaverkill Road
Lew Beach, NY 12753

Yellow Breeches Sporting
   Outfitters
Box 417
Boiling Springs, PA 17007
Ed Shenk and Joe Humphreys

Yellowstone Angler
124 North Main Street
Livingston, MT 59047
George Anderson and Steve
   Rajeff

ANTIQUE TACKLE DEALERS

Believe it or not, antique rods, reels, and lures are fetching thousands of dollars on the collectors' circuit. Fishing tackle has entered the realm of high-return investment, particularly where antique fly tackle is concerned. While we would not suggest investing in antique tackle without a detailed understanding of market conditions, examining and studying older varieties of tackle is fascinating for many anglers. There's probably a dealer near you; pay him a visit one weekend just to look at his stuff. You'll find it hard to believe that some of these things caught fish.

Antique Fishing Collectibles,
   Inc.
Antique Fishing Collectibles
   Newsletter
Alexander XX
P.O. Box 627
Newtown, PA 18940

The Bedford Sportsman Inc.
Depot Plaza
Bedford IIills, NY 10507

Hoagy Carmichael
Guard Hill Road
Bedford, NY 10506

Thomas H. Clark
1208 W. Washington
Jackson, MI 49203

J. Garman
887 Main Street
Manchester, CT 06040

Frederick E. Grafeld
297 Born St.
Secaucus, NJ 07094

Martin J. Keane
P.O. Box 888
Stockbridge, MA 01262

National Fishing Lure
   Collectors Club
NFLCC Gazette
3907 Wedgewood Drive
Portage, MI 49008

Thomas & Thomas
22 Third Street
P.O. Box 32
Turners Falls, MA 01376

Vintage Rod & Reel
Box 127
Talent, OR 97540

FOOTNOTES

1. Vlad Evanoff, THE FRESH-WATER FISHERMAN'S BIBLE (Garden City, New York: Doubleday & Co., 1964).

2. A.J. McClane, MCCLANE'S SECRETS OF SUCCESSFUL FISHING (New York: Henry Holt & Co., 1979).

3. Ibid.

4. Mike Rosenthal, NORTH AMERICA'S FRESHWATER FISHING BOOK (New York: Scribner's & Sons, 1983).

5. Ibid.

6. Gary Soucie, HOOK, LINE AND SINKER (New York: Holt, Rhinehart & Winston, 1982; Simon & Schuster/Fireside, 1988).

7. Ibid.

8. Ibid.

9. Ibid.

10. A.J. McClane, MCCLANE'S SECRETS OF SUCCESSFUL FISHING, (New York, Henry Holt & Co., 1979).

11. Gary Soucie, HOOK, LINE AND SINKER (New York: Holt, Rhinehart & Winston, 1982; Simon & Schuster/Fireside, 1988).

12. Ibid.

13. Keith Gardner, Editor, THE COMPLETE BOOK OF FISHING (New York: W.H. Smith, 1987).

14. Gary Soucie, HOOK, LINE AND SINKER (New York: Holt, Rhinehart & Winston, 1982; Simon & Schuster/Fireside, 1988).

15. Keith Gardner, Editor, THE COMPLETE BOOK OF FISHING (New York: W.H. Smith, 1987).

16. Gary Soucie, HOOK, LINE AND SINKER (New York: Holt, Rhinehart & Winston, 1982; Simon & Schuster/Fireside, 1988).

17. Ibid.

18. Ibid.

19. A.J. McClane, FIELD GUIDE TO SALTWATER FISHES OF NORTH AMERICA (New York: Henry Holt & Co., 1974).

20. Gary Soucie, HOOK, LINE AND SINKER (New York: Holt, Rhinehart & Winston, 1982; Simon & Schuster/Fireside, 1988).

21. Ibid.

22. Ibid.

23. Erwin A. Bauer, THE SALTWATER FISHERMAN'S BIBLE (Garden City, New York: Doubleday & Co., 1983).

24. Ibid.

25. Scott Roederer, THE COMPLETE ANGLER'S CATALOG (Boulder, Colorado: Johnson Books/Spring Creek Press, 1985).

26. Ibid.

27. Ibid.

28. Ibid.

29. Lee Wulff, TROUT ON A FLY (New York: Nick Lyons Books, 1986).

30. Scott Roederer, THE COMPLETE ANGLER'S CATALOG (Boulder, Colorado: Johnson Books/Spring Creek Press, 1985).

31. Ibid.

32. John Buckland, THE SIMON AND SCHUSTER GUIDE TO TROUT AND SALMON FLIES (New York: Simon & Schuster/Fireside, 1987).

33. Ray Bergman, TROUT (New York: Alfred A. Knopf, 1987).

34. Ibid.

35. Art Flick, THE STREAMSIDE GUIDE TO NATURALS AND THEIR IMITATIONS (New York: Nick Lyons Books, 1985).

36. Paul Schullery, AMERICAN FLY FISH-ING: A History (New York: Nick Lyons Books, 1987).

37. Ray Bergman, TROUT (New York: Alfred A. Knopf, 1987).

38. Paul Schullery, AMERICAN FLY FISH-ING: A History (New York: Nick Lyons Books, 1987).

INDEX

SILHOUETTED PHOTOGRAPHS